# The Righteousness of One

# The Righteousness of One

An Evaluation of Early Patristic Soteriology
in Light of the New Perspective on Paul

JORDAN COOPER

WIPF & STOCK · Eugene, Oregon

THE RIGHTEOUSNESS OF ONE
An Evaluation of Early Patristic Soteriology in Light of the New Perspective on Paul

Copyright © 2013 Jordan Cooper. All rights reserved. Except for brief quotations in critical publications or reviews, no part of this book may be reproduced in any manner without prior written permission from the publisher. Write: Permissions, Wipf and Stock Publishers, 199 W. 8th Ave., Suite 3, Eugene, OR 97401.

Wipf & Stock
An imprint of Wipf and Stock Publishers
199 W. 8th Ave., Suite 3
Eugene, OR 97401

www.wipfandstock.com

ISBN 13: 978-1-62032-758-6

Manufactured in the U.S.A.

*"To my wife, who is so helpful and patient;
she spent long hours editing this work,
and gave me direction in my research."*

# Contents

*Foreword* / ix

1   The New Perspective on Paul / 1

2   Methodology / 16

3   Previous Research on Patristic Soteriology / 27

4   Which Luther / 40

5   The Apostolic Fathers / 68

6   Justin Martyr / 98

7   Conclusion / 121

*Bibliography* / 137

# Foreword

SUBSTANTIVELY, THE LITERATURE PUBLISHED under the rubric "New Perspective on Paul" is always provocative, and I consider some of its central claims compelling. The marketing of the New Perspective, however, has been less persuasive.

To convince consumers of the freshness of their approach, New Perspective writers set their views in opposition to traditional interpretations of Paul. Stendahl's Luther of the Anguished Conscience has been the bogeyman the New Perspective uses to frighten small children. Behind Luther looms Augustine, the poisoned spring from which individualistic Western soteriologies flow.

This is not historically plausible. Like Origen and Jerome, Augustine anticipated themes of the New Perspective. In Letter 82, he describes the debate in Galatia as a battle about how to induct Gentiles into the people of God. Paul's circumcision of Timothy was legitimate because "these rites and traditions [of Judaism] were not harmful to people born and raised in that way." Those who came from outside, however, "were bound by no such requirement but came as it were from the opposite wall, that is, from those without circumcision, to that cornerstone, which is Christ." Entering through a different door, they "were forced into no such rites." Controversy broke out because "certain wicked people persuaded [Gentiles] that they could not be saved without these works of the law," while Paul insisted that they did not need to be "burdened by any such observances" so that Christ could not be obscured by "such unheard-of practices, especially circumcision." It's enough to make James Dunn's face shine.

Though he is more skeptical of the New Perspective than I, Jordan Cooper provides a much-needed historical ground clearing. Drawing on recent Luther scholarship, he shows that New Perspective caricatures of Luther do not hold up. Carefully analyzing a wealth of early evidence, he demonstrates convincingly that Luther's concern for individual salvation and his accent on faith operate well within patristic parameters. Throughout, Cooper writes with disarming honesty, resisting the Procrustean temptation to stretch or scrunch church fathers into Lutheran shape.

Cooper's book should have a dramatic effect on the debate, since I suspect opponents recoil as much from New Perspective marketing as from New Perspective substance. We know what the decision will be if a Lutheran is told to choose between Luther and N. T. Wright.

Cooper does not claim to pass final judgment on the New Perspective. What he offers is the opportunity to renew the debate in a more historically informed fashion. Having cleared the clutter, Cooper leaves us still with the task of grasping what St. Paul really said.

Peter J. Leithart
Peniel Hall
Moscow, Idaho
Trinity Season 2012

# 1

# The New Perspective on Paul

## INTRODUCTION TO THE PROBLEM

AT THE BEGINNING OF the twenty-first century, the subject of justification has once again come to the forefront of much theological dialogue. Perhaps not since the Reformation of the sixteenth century has such an extensive dialogue arisen around the doctrine of justification by faith. In the modern ecumenical age, however, these dialogues are not concentrated in Roman Catholic and Protestant polemics, but in the realm of Pauline studies.

The latter half of the twentieth century saw a major shift in Pauline studies, particularly in Paul's relation to Judaism and the law. From the sixteenth century throughout much of the twentieth, Martin Luther's interpretation of Paul was widely accepted by most within Protestantism. While not necessarily affirming every nuance of Luther's interpretation, exegetes had accepted his basic premise that Paul, in his epistles to the Galatians and Romans, was fighting against Jewish legalism of sorts.

## The Righteousness of One

The so-called New Perspective on Paul[1] has challenged the validity of the Reformation reading of Paul, insisting that Martin Luther's tortured conscience may have had a larger role in his interpretation of Paul than careful, honest, exegetical study. Luther is of course, not the only culprit regarding an individualistic, introspective reading of Paulinism. It is the Augustinian dominance of Western theology that is to blame.

The "Lutheran Paul" of the West stressed justification by faith alone as the center of his gospel. This doctrine was ultimately aimed at the comforting of the conscience of the man, who, being struck by the perfection required in God's holy law, needed a means of forgiveness. This idea of Paulinism was certainly not universal, as men like Herman Ridderbos[2] found the center of Paul's thought not in justification, but in the broader theme of union with Christ. The "Lutheran Paul" found its ultimate expression in the writings of Rudolph Bultmann. Bultmann, using existentialist philosophy as a backdrop, saw Paul as answering the plight of every person, which emphasizes the complete dependence of man upon God, and God's act of bringing about an open future. His personalized eschatology was not rooted in the historical figure of Jesus, but in an existential principle. Paul spoke unilateral truth, not necessarily grounded within history.[3] Paul distanced himself from the Judaism of his past, seeing it as nothing more than pure legalism. In Judaism, God weighed one's merits against his

---

1. Henceforth, this will often be referred to as the "NPP."

2. Ridderbos, *Paul*.

3. That is, he rejects history in the sense of objective study of events in the past. For Bultmann, the gospel is historical in a different sense. It affects one's personal history, wherein one is brought out of inauthentic, sinful existence, into the eschatological reality of an open future through the Christ event. A full treatment of this can be found in Bultmann, *Presence of Eternity*.

*The New Perspective on Paul*

demerits in order to determine final salvation. Bultmann emphasized the distinction between the law and the gospel farther than Martin Luther himself would have imagined, and interpreted them through the lens of Heideggerian[4] and neo-Kantian[5] philosophy. Luther saw the law and the gospel as both given by God, present in the Old and New Testaments, and as good things that both aimed at the salvation of God's people. The law showed the need for salvation, and the gospel provided it. Other writers saw Paul as much more consistent with historical events and his Jewish past, as even Bultmann's student Gunther Bornkamm[6] showed the necessity of the historical person of Jesus in Paul's theology while agreeing with Bultmann on the centrality of the doctrine of justification in Paul's thought. W. D. Davies[7] showed convincingly that Paul's theology was largely influenced by Judaism and that the break between Paul and Judaism was not as great as many had assumed it to be.

## KRISTER STENDHAL

In 1963, Krister Stendhal published an influential article that challenged previous views of Paul and his relation to the law.[8] Stendhal argued that since the Reformation interpreters have read Luther's experience back into the writings of Paul, rather than comprehending Paul on his own terms. Our conception of Paul is a product of medieval thought

---

4. A thorough treatment of Heidegger's influence on Bultmann can be found in MacQuarrie, *Existentialist Theology*.

5. A defense of neo-Kantian influence in Bultmann's thought is convincingly given in Dennison, *Young Bultmann*.

6. Bornkamm, *Paul*.

7. Davies, *Paul and Rabbinic Judaism*.

8. Stendahl, "Apostle Paul and the Introspective Conscience of the West."

in the Western world that would have been completely foreign to those in the period of Second Temple Judaism. Paul himself did not have a troubled conscience as did Augustine, Luther, or Wesley. He in fact had a "robust conscience."[9] In Philippians Paul described his former life in Judaism as one of "blamelessness," not of a failing struggle to obey the law. When Paul talks of the perfect obedience required in the law, it has a more corporate than individual meaning. The nation of Israel as a whole failed to keep the law that was required of them, as Paul describes in Romans 2. Paul's discussions about the failure of the law are not to provoke the conscience of his readers, but are aimed at defining the relationship between Jew and Gentile.

It has been assumed that Paul's experience on the Damascus road was a conversion to a new way of life. He was a Jew who struggled to obey the whole law, realized he could not, and then converted to faith in Christ. This idea comes from the autobiographical reading of Romans 7. On the contrary, Stendhal believes, "There is not—as we usually think—first a conversion, then a call to apostleship; there is only the call to work among the gentiles."[10] Paul's break from Judaism was not much of a break at all, but instead it was a new understanding. Paul's purpose from this point forward was to work out the relation between Jewish Christians and Gentile Christians. For Luther, Calvin, and other exegetes, chapters 3 and 4were the central discussion of Paul's epistle to the Romans. The theme was seen as the righteousness of God expressed in justification. This incidentally led to the discussion of the relationship between Jew and Gentile in chapters 11. On the contrary, according to Stendhal, the center of Paul's epistle to the Romans is chapters 9–11. The discussion of justification served only as a backdrop for this

9. Ibid., 80
10. Ibid., 84–85.

part of Paul's argument. The protestant idea of justification is a non-historical one that sees Paul's doctrine as addressing a universal problem for men of all times, rather than understanding the context of Paul preaching to a Jewish audience of the Messiah. The law Paul speaks of is the Mosaic law given to Israel, not a set of universal rules to be obeyed by everyone. The so-called "second use of the law" as applied to converting all men, Jew and Gentile alike, to faith in Christ is a complete misuse of Paul.

Though denying the Lutheran emphasis on the law's second use, Stendahl confesses that Paul does emphasize sin in his epistles. When he writes of his own sin, he is not discussing his burdened conscience. Rather, he speaks of the sin of persecuting the church of God, which he had now made up for. All of this does not mean that Paul held the view that after baptism man becomes sinless; he accepts that Christians do struggle. However, the focus of his discussion of struggle is not one of despair, but of victory over that sin. After his so-called conversion, Paul was not troubled in his conscience, as he testifies in Acts 23:1 among other places. He does speak of "weakness" as the thorn in the flesh, but these weaknesses are unconnected to indwelling sin. Stendahl asserts, "But there is no indication that Paul ever thought of this and his other 'weaknesses' as sins for which he was responsible."[11]

## E. P. SANDERS

E. P. Sanders drew upon Stendahl's article in his monumental book *Paul and Palestinian Judaism*.[12] In this work, Sanders evaluates common Protestant understandings of

11. Ibid., 91.
12. Sanders, *Paul and Palestinian Judaism*.

# The Righteousness of One

Second Temple Judaism. According to Sanders, these works share a common flaw in assuming legalism in Jewish theology. This happens because Protestant readers read Luther's controversy with the medieval church into Paul's polemical writings against the Judaizers. According to Sanders, Second Temple Jewish sources can be broadly placed under the rubric he labels "covenantal nomism." In covenantal nomism, one is a member of the covenant by grace. God selected Israel as his people by grace alone, and works play no role in being born of a Jewish family. Works then serve to maintain one's status in God's covenant family, never to earn grace.[13] Jews of the first century were not proto-Pelagians. Thus, for Sanders, Second Temple Judaism is not the religion of works righteousness that Luther assumed it to be, but a religion of grace.[14]

Like Stendahl, Sander's thesis is ultimately an attack on Luther's reading of Paul. Ultimately, Luther forced his own situation within the medieval church into the writings of Paul. Paul was not fighting against Jewish legalism in defense of *sola gratia*. This could not be the case due to the fact that Jewish legalism did not exist in the first century. Thus the entire Reformation tradition is based upon anachronism.

---

13. With the exception of 4 *Ezra*, which Sanders admits teaches works righteousness.

14. This begs the question as to whether a system wherein one must obey the law to maintain a status in the covenant cannot also be labeled "works righteousness." After all, the medieval Roman church did teach entrance into the covenant by grace through baptism. Ironically Sanders' treatment indicates more commonality with the medieval Roman tradition fought against by Luther than previous studies had indicated.

*The New Perspective on Paul*

## JAMES DUNN

James Dunn is the third major writer within this blossoming tradition of Pauline interpretation.[15] Dunn is the first writer to produce commentaries of Paul's epistles through this framework, and also formulated the term "the new perspective on Paul." Dunn essentially agrees with Sanders' assessment of Second Temple Judaism as a religion of grace rather than merit. Dunn likewise criticizes Luther for reading medievalism into the Pauline corpus. However, Dunn views the earlier two writers as inadequate: "I am not convinced that we have yet given the proper reading of Paul from the new perspective of first-century Palestinian Judaism opened up so helpfully by Sanders himself."[16]

Dunn formulates a differing interpretation of Romans and Galatians. His argument hinges upon Galatians 2:16, which is, according to Dunn, the earliest explicit reference to the doctrine of justification in the Pauline corpus. In this passage, Paul is addressing the issue of table fellowship between Jew and Gentile. Justification was viewed as the property of Jews but not Gentiles. This is apparent in Paul's labeling them, rhetorically, as "sinners." Paul argues against this notion, demonstrating the universal nature of justification by faith. Dunn rejects Luther's belief that justification is a term describing the beginning of a man's relation toward God: "Justification is rather God's acknowledgement that one is in the covenant-whether that is an *initial* acknowledgment, or a *repeated* action of God (God's saving acts), or his *final* vindication of his people."[17] For Dunn, Paul is

15. Dunn's essays on the issue have been compiled in Dunn, *New Perspective on Paul*.

16. Ibid., 95.

17. Ibid., 97. This seems to neglect the richness of Luther's writing on justification in favor of a scholastic doctrine of justification, which Dunn assumes to represent the real Luther. This will be shown to be

working within an explicitly Jewish framework. Those who Paul is countering in Galatia view their Christianity as an extension of Judaism. As such, justification by faith is a Jewish teaching understood by his Jewish readers. Both Judaism and Christianity approach salvation as an act of grace.

Dunn, accepting Sanders' critique that Paul was not arguing against Jewish legalism, writes that "works of the Law" in Paul refer to "works related to the covenant [and] works done in obedience to the covenant."[18] Thus, when Paul speaks of works of the law he does not refer to good works in general, or even good works as conforming to the Decalogue. These works are primarily those that separate Jews from Gentiles, which would include the Sabbath, food laws, and other boundary markers that differentiated Jew from Gentile. The phrase "works of the law" itself is nationalistic in focus: "The law and the Jewish people are coterminous; the law identifies the Jew as Jew and constitutes the boundary which separates him from the gentiles."[19]

Paul does not invalidate the covenantal nomistic soteriology of the Judaism of his day. However, he redefines this in light of the resurrected messiah. The question Paul needed to deal with was, "How do we Jewish believers relate our Covenantal Nomism, our works of the law, our obligations under the covenant to our new faith in Jesus as the

---

flawed in chapter 4 below.

18. Ibid., 98.

19. Ibid., 118. It amazes me that this is often seen as a profound discovery within Pauline scholarship when it simply goes back to the debate between Jerome and Augustine over the interpretation of the phrase "works of the law." These issues were also dealt with at length during the sixteenth and seventeenth centuries, when many Roman Catholics took a similar view to Dunn on this point. The lack of historical theology within the discussion leaves a gaping chasm in the contemporary Pauline dialogue.

*The New Perspective on Paul*

Christ?"[20] The elect were, in the national covenant, those who had the marks of circumcision, food laws, Sabbath, etc. After Christ, Paul reformulates election around those who have faith. The mark or badge of that covenant identity is now faith in Christ only.

Like the other writers embracing this new understanding of Paul, Dunn argues that the law/gospel or faith/works contrast as traditionally understood within Lutheran readings is wrong. "Paul is not arguing here for a concept of faith which is totally passive because it fears to become a 'work.'"[21] Dunn also argues that there is not a necessary dichotomy between ritual and faith. He is not arguing against ritual as such, but that which excludes Gentiles from the covenant. "What he is concerned to exclude here is the racial, not the ritual expression of faith; it is *nationalism* he denies not *activism*."[22] What is new about the covenant, according to Paul, is not that now an alternative to legalistic works has appeared, making salvation a matter of passive faith, but that Gentiles are now included within God's people.

## N. T. WRIGHT

Bishop N. T. Wright, one of the most prominent New Testament scholars of today, did much to bring this "new perspective" to a popular audience. His volume *What Saint Paul Really Said*,[23] released in 1997, is a compact treatment of Paul's beliefs as influenced by expectations of the Second Temple period. Wright accepts the general categorization of

20. Ibid., 103.
21. Ibid., 105.
22. Ibid.
23. Wright, *What Saint Paul Really Said*.

Second Temple texts within the framework of "covenantal nomism." Wright argues that because Luther's reading of Paul has become standard, a fresh and honest reading of the Pauline material has been hampered.

For Wright, Paul is essentially working within a narrative structure.[24] This narrative is the story of God's dealings with man through Israel, now fulfilled through the coming of Christ. God created Adam as the first of all humanity to live in obedience to himself. Adam rebelled, as did all men after him. This is the beginning of the story. God called out Abraham so that he might be a light to the world and undo the problem that came through the sin in the garden. "The canonical Old Testament frames the entire story of God's people as the divine answer to the problem of evil: somehow, through his people, God will deal with the problem that has effected his good creation in general and his image-bearing creatures in general."[25] Israel is chosen out of pure grace, and is given the Torah and temple as a means toward redemption. However, rather than fixing the problem of sin and evil in the world, Israel became a part of the problem.

Wright promotes the idea that when the exile in Babylon ended, and the Israelites were brought back into the land, the majority of Jews still believed themselves in exile. Wright particularly defends this thesis in his 1991 volume *The Climax of the Covenant*.[26] Israel, after the exile, had not gained all of the land that was expected by the prophets. They were still under foreign oppressors. The real ending of the exile would occur when Israel once again became an autonomous nation, and God directly ruled over them through a Davidic king. This idea was in Paul's mind when

---

24. Wright's interpretive methodology, which he labels "critical realism," can be found in Wright, *New Testament and the People of God*.

25. Wright, *Paul in Fresh Perspective*, 109.

26. Wright, *Climax of the Covenant*.

*The New Perspective on Paul*

he wrote his epistle to the Galatians. Galatians 3:10 has historically been used to promote the doctrine of penal substitution. The curse Christ paid for was the penalty of breaking God's perfect law. Wright takes this verse in a different direction by seeing the curse for which Christ paid as the exile. Through the death and resurrection of Christ, Israel's exile has finally come to an end. The kingdom has been inaugurated.

Perhaps Wright's most controversial contribution to Pauline theology is his attack on the Protestant definition of justification as promoted by Martin Luther. He contends, along with Stendhal and Dunn, that Paul was not fighting against legalism in Galatians and Romans. The justification by works that Paul writes against is not "individual Jews attempting a kind of proto-Pelagian pulling themselves up by their moral bootstraps."[27] Rather, it is that Jews excluded Gentiles from fellowship within the kingdom. Justification for Paul is a legal term. However, it is not a term about "getting in," but it is a term about "who is in" the covenant. Wright argues, "Justification in Galatians, is the doctrine which insists that all who share faith in Christ belong to the same table, no matter what their racial differences, as together they wait for the final creation."[28] When God declares one to be justified, he is declaring them to be among his people. It does not involve the imputation of righteousness. "If we use the language of law court, it makes no sense whatever to say the judge imparts, imputes, bequeaths, conveys or otherwise transfers his righteousness to either plaintiff or the defendant."[29]

For Wright, the righteousness of God is his covenant faithfulness. It is not an abstract attribute that all men are

27. Wright, *What Saint Paul Really Said*, 119.
28. Ibid., 122.
29. Ibid., 98.

required to live up to. It is not something to be imputed to man. It is his faithfulness in dealing with and saving his people. This underlies Wright's redefinition of justification. It is founded in the Jewish idea of covenant. This is why several psalmists are able to ask God to deliver them in his righteousness. In this context it certainly means deliverance, not imputation.

## RESPONDING TO THE NEW PERSPECTIVE

There have been several responses to the NPP since its rise in popularity. From Gunther Bornkamm's *Paul* to A. Andrew Das' *Paul, the Law, and Covenant*, responses to Stendahl, Sanders, Dunn, and Wright have reevaluated Paul's writings and the Second Temple Jewish sources drawn upon by Sanders.[30] This has often been accomplished by demonstrating that Second Temple Judaism, though partially gracious, has several elements of legalism inherent in its system, and by thorough exegesis of Paul's epistles. Though several writers have defended a Lutheran reading of Paul, not many detractors have been convinced. As helpful as many of these responses have been, they have largely ignored an essential aspect of Stendahl's argument: the realm of historical theology.

The centuries immediately preceding Paul are a valuable resource for understanding Paul's conceptual world and terminology; however, a study of the immediate post-apostolic commentators on Pauline justification has been neglected. This deficiency in Pauline scholarship has

---

30. Some responses to the new perspective can be found in: Das, *Paul, the Law and Covenant*; Carson et al., *Justification and Variegated Nomism*; Schreiner, *Law and Its Fulfillment*; Piper, *Future of Justification;* Seifrid, *Christ Our Righteousness*; Gathercole, *Where Is Boasting?*; and Thielman, *Paul & the Law.*

divorced Paul from the post-apostolic interpretive community that received his texts. Because the second-century church's historical and theological context approximates Paul's more closely than our own, the testimony of Paul's earliest interpreters should function as a hermeneutical guide for continuity of thought and consistency with Luther's teaching on justification. An exegetical analysis of these early writers, in conversation with Luther, will establish the fact that Luther himself was more consistent with the inherited tradition of Paul than Stendahl, Wright, and other NPP proponents.

Another work on justification, the law, and Second Temple Judaism in Paul's thought may seem superfluous, as the overabundance of material on these subjects has often garbled, rather than clarified the issues. Interpretations of Paul have become nearly as numerous as Pauline interpreters. Thankfully, this is not another work on the theology of Paul. Perhaps it is due to the unfortunate division between historical and exegetical theology in a specialized age, or perhaps due to the assumption that the Western church simply had no soteriology before Augustine—but whatever the reason, Paul's earliest interpreters have been left out of the discussion.

Since the modern discussions of Paul began with a statement about historical theology—namely that the Augustinian tradition, especially as interpreted by Luther, is wrong—historical theology has a necessary place in the contemporary Pauline dialogue. For the criticisms of Stendahl, Wright, and Dunn to have validity, two historical truths must be established that are often presupposed rather than defended: first, that the introspective, individualistic Luther, who regards justification as a purely legal transfer term, being critiqued is an accurate picture of the reformer; second, that the Augustinian reading of Paul is the beginning of an understanding of Paulinism concerned with individual salvation. Before Augustine, accord to the NPP, Paul was understood as dealing with the specific issue of Jew-Gentile relations in the new covenant rather than the relationship between good works and faith for an individual's salvation. If these two premises are wrong, Stendahl's thesis must be reevaluated to fit the historical reality.

It is my contention that both of these premises are indeed flawed. Luther's theology has often been caricatured by New Testament scholars who assume that later scholastic or even pietistic and existential readings of Luther accurately represent the reformer. This then divorces Luther from the patristic sources with whom he often agrees. While Augustine brought soteriological discussions to the forefront of theological discussion, these issues are far from absent in the pre-Augustinian church. There is a significant amount of material in earlier church fathers regarding Paul's epistles to the Romans and Galatians, as well as a concern for individual salvation.

I propose that Luther's view of justification is not new. Contrary to the claim that he is simply a child of a medieval obsession with personal salvation, Luther is an honest and perceptive student of Paul. Not only medieval figures, but the earliest Pauline interpreters understood Paul in a "Lutheran" manner. This is not to say that the earliest Christians were consistent Lutherans, but simply that in many aspects they interpreted Paul in a similar fashion. This shows that a medieval context is not necessary for Luther's primary soteriological themes.

This will be demonstrated through a study of Luther's doctrine of justification. Luther's theology must be presented accurately to correct the caricature presented by Stendahl, Dunn, and Wright. It will be shown that Luther does not defend justification as a purely legal concept and

## The New Perspective on Paul

as only a transfer term, while ignoring the rest of Pauline soteriological concerns. His thought is also not purely reactionary against medieval semi-Pelagianism, but takes both the Pauline epistles and patristic interpretation seriously. Secondly, I will analyze the earliest Pauline interpreters in light of both Luther and the NPP. This will be done through a study of the apostolic fathers and Justin Martyr. Do the early Christian's view the Pauline polemic as an attack on works righteousness, or as an attempt to solve a purely ecclesial problem? I contend that there is more "Lutheranism" in the earliest readings of Paul's epistles than the NPP proponents are willing to admit.

This book does not propose to be the definitive work on the NPP, but it is an attempt to enter the dialogue where voices have been significantly absent. Hopefully a new (or old) understanding of both the early church and Paul will be nurtured in the following pages.

# 2

# Methodology

## MY ASSUMPTIONS ABOUT PAUL

As I begin this study, I must lay forth my assumptions about the Pauline canon and Pauline theology as I understand them from previous study. When I speak of Pauline literature, I accept the traditional attribution of the thirteen epistles to Paul—yes, even the pastorals.[1] Thus, when I speak of Pauline interpretation, I refer to hermeneutics that deal with all thirteen epistles attributed to the apostle. However, the bulk of the discussion revolves around the undisputed epistles, primarily Galatians and Romans, so that those who do not adhere to the traditional Pauline canon should not be put off by this study.

Regarding Paul's message, I accept the traditional Lutheran interpretive grid. I think that a law/gospel

---

1. I have been convinced of much that is defended in Robinson, *Redating the New Testament*. He demonstrates that early dating of the Pauline epistles is historically tenable despite what many interpreters, following Baur, and less so Harnack, have taken for granted.

*Methodology*

distinction does exist in Paulinism despite the claims of the NPP. Westerholm's *Perspectives on Paul: The "Lutheran" Paul and His Critics* has been decisive for me in this regard.² Westerholm demonstrates that a law/gospel dialectic exists in the Pauline writings. The law is not purely an issue of ceremonial works or civic duty, but of God's moral command. Paul, especially in Galatians 3–4, contrasts this with the Abrahamic promise in a manner commensurate with the law/gospel hermeneutic of Luther. While the NPP certainly has pointed toward an aspect of Paulinism that has sometimes been neglected due to the polemical context of which these discussions are often a part, it is my contention that a minor point in Paulinism has now been accepted as his sole concern. Paul's views on covenant fellowship between Jews and Gentiles are certainly important, but remain a secondary issue. To invert a favorite analogy of Tom Wright, the NPP authors have taken the minor point of ethnic identity and expanded upon it as the issue around which every other Pauline theme revolves. It is a case of assuming that the sun revolves around the earth rather than vice versa. In Lutheran Pauline interpretation (which I believe to be correct), the center of Pauline theology is God's act in Christ on behalf of sinners. The issue of table fellowship is merely one of the many issues revolving around this center.

    I also accept Luther's approach to the law as having a much broader definition than Mosaic Torah.³ Paul brings the discussion in Romans back to the garden of Eden, establishing νομοσ. as a creational category, rather than simply Jewish boundary markers. For Paul, the law has brought

---

    2. Wright's criticisms of Westerholm in *Justification* have failed to overthrow the thrust of Westerholm's argument.

    3. The best defense of this idea is found in Vlachos, *Law and the Knowledge of Good and Evil*, wherein he demonstrates that law for Paul is a creational rather than purely covenantal category.

about death for Adam and Eve. It has done the same ever since.[4] The role of the law is to expose sin and condemn the world before God. Christ is the solution to this problem, dying, rising from the dead, and uniting himself to his people through baptism, and consequently God justifies sinners because of the righteousness of Jesus Christ.[5] I do, however, believe that the NPP authors, specifically Wright, have brought a renewed emphasis on the resurrection as essential to Paul's concept of justification, which has been lost in the Reformation tradition. As I will demonstrate below, Luther emphasizes the resurrection far more robustly than the following tradition in the West.

## PATRISTIC THEOLOGY AND HERMENEUTICS

Before undertaking an evaluation of the teachings of Luther and the early church, something must be said about the issue of hermeneutics and patristic biblical interpretation. For this study to have legitimacy, patristic theology must have some validity as a lens through which one can gain understanding of the New Testament text.

The twentieth century experienced a fundamental shift in philosophical discourse from the area of metaphysics and

---

4. I think that there is an Edenic illusion in the much-debated discussion in Romans 7. However, I don't think that this negates the fact that Paul is speaking of himself in the present tense. He is presenting himself as one who is in the same situation as Adam. Like Adam, he is given a law to obey, and like Adam he fails and brings death to himself.

5. An exegetical defense I have found to be thoroughly convincing of imputed righteousness is Vicars, Jesus' Blood and Righteousness. Vicars demonstrates that though no single verse in Paul states that God imputes us righteous through faith by the righteousness of Christ, putting together several trajectories in his thought demonstrate that this is his conviction.

*Methodology*

epistemology to that of language and hermeneutics.[6] The modern (and often premodern) assumption that one can approach a text from an objective standpoint has been challenged through the growth of postmodernism. According to postmodern hermeneutics, there is no God's-eye view on a text, but one approaches any reading with one's own presuppositions and biases. This transition has affected not only the realm of literary theory and philosophy, but has raised new questions for Christian theology.

Christianity must approach truth with the affirmation of objective truth. As Barth reminded the church so profoundly, veracity is found in revelation—Christ himself. However, even if the Christian has an answer to a relativist conception of truth in Jesus Christ, the question of hermeneutics still stands. The question is not new. Protestant and Roman Catholic polemics have engaged the question of biblical interpretation for years. For the Roman Catholic, Scripture was explained as an obscure book. It does not in itself give enough information or clarity for the understanding and propagation of dogma; thus an infallible magisterium is necessary for proper exegesis.[7] The Protestant polemicist, whether Lutheran or Reformed, responded with a defense of the perspicuity of the sacred text, establishing the *sola scriptura* principle.[8]

---

6. Wittgenstein and the rise of postmodernity are the two primary factors in this shift. In Christian theology these issues have gained prominence through the writings of Barth, the "post-liberal" tradition as explicated by George Lindbeck and Brevard Childs, and more recently Kevin VanHoozer. For an introduction to these issues see VanHoozer, *Is There a Meaning in This Text?*

7. And of course, modern Roman Catholic writers have defended this view as well. For example: Sungenis, *Not by Scripture Alone*.

8. There are many modern defenses of sola scriptura as well such as: White, *Scripture Alone*; and King and Webster, *Holy Scripture*.

## The Righteousness of One

In the contemporary ecclesiological situation, the principle of *sola scriptura* has often devolved into *nuda scriptura*. Scripture is treated as a sole authority to the neglect of all teachers, councils, confessions, and church traditions. Due to the influence of pietistic individualism in the West, as well as a prevailing historical ignorance, many Christians have adopted the objectivist naivety that prevailed in the modernist period. Scripture has been divorced from its interpretive community, leaving Christians to rehash debates that were resolved in centuries past, supposing that they may approach the scriptures anew without bias.

During the sixteenth-century Reformation, the situation was much different. Both Calvin's[9] and Luther's writings are drenched in patristic and medieval quotations. Though patrology gradually became less common in Reformed thought,[10] the Lutheran tradition continually preserved the importance of the Church's historical continuity. The Lutheran confessions defend their doctrinal assertions with patristic quotations along with biblical exegesis; this is not the case with the Reformed confessions. Martin Chemnitz continued this tradition with his Examination of the Council of Trent, claiming that several patristic sources agreed with the Lutheran Reformation over against the claims of Rome.

For Chemnitz, as well as the other Lutheran reformers, historical continuity is not a perennial issue. It is an essential part of the dogmatic task. Without any patristic defense on a major doctrinal point, that doctrinal claim

---

9. See for example Calvin's *Bondage and Liberation of the Will*, in which his mastery of Augustine's thought is apparent.

10. This was not universally the case. John Owen, for example, was quite fond of Aquinas, and Augustine's voice was never silenced regarding divine predestination. Richard Muller also notes several instances of similarity between patristic, medieval, and Reformed scholastic theology in his four-volume *Post-Reformation Reformed Dogmatics*.

*Methodology*

itself is put into doubt. This principle extends through the scholastic period of the seventeenth century, as is evident from Johann Gerhard's *Confessio Catholica*, wherein Lutheran doctrine is thoroughly examined through the lens of patristic theology.

In the postmodern situation, this historical consciousness is ever more needed. One need not flee to the claim of an infallible interpreter, or retreat to hermeneutical relativism, to interact with the truth of reader subjectivity. What is needed is the consciousness that Scripture is, as is any other important literary work, not only the product of a historical situation, but also a text received by an interpretive community. This interpretive community need not be seen as a hindrance to comprehending the author's original intent (one would then be reverting back to the modernist concept that the modern reader's interpretive grid is more "objective" than that of the text's more immediate audience), but as a guiding light, challenging our own biases and assumptions about the text and enlightening that which may seem obscure to the modern reader.[11]

This approach to Scripture takes reader subjectivity and bias seriously by placing an interpretive grid over the text, while affirming that genuine knowledge and understanding can be gained from the reading of Scripture apart from an infallible magisterium. This is not a rejection of *sola scriptura*, but an affirmation of its original intent. Scripture is the only infallible means of Christian revelation, but it has been interpreted by the Spirit-empowered Christian community, and the interpretation of this community needs to be taken seriously.

---

11. I affirm much of what Wright defends as "critical realism" in *The New Testament and the People of God*. The role of the interpretive community, however, has been neglected here.

## SOURCES

The question naturally arises as to which patristic sources should be evaluated in this study. If patristic theology serves as a valid hermeneutical grid, which sources should have primacy? Should an agreement be sought with all early Christian sources?

From Vincent of Lerins to the Council of Trent, from George Calixtus to Thomas Oden, many authors have tried to argue for an "orthodox consensus" of the faith of the early church. In this approach there may not be agreement on every distinct Christian doctrine, but there is a strand of unchangeable truth within the patristic tradition (at least those generally considered to be orthodox). I find this approach somewhat naïve. Though there are similarities throughout orthodox patristic texts, I do not find that such a unified tradition exists. Even among those generally considered orthodox, there is no agreement, for example, as to the nature of Christ's preexistence.[12] What is being sought therefore is a strand of patristic theology, not its unified stance.

For the sake of beginning the discussion, I have chosen to focus on the earliest Christian writers who interact with Pauline themes. This is not to assume that these four writers represent the only form of Christian orthodoxy in the first two centuries, nor is it even to say that they agree among themselves. However, they are four sources that

12. The two common approaches to Christ's preexistence are not the Arian and orthodox, but the one- and two-stage theories. In the one-stage theory (such as in Irenaeus) Christ was a preexistent person with God the Father in eternity past. In the two-stage theory (most popularly explained by Justin and adopted by many of the second-century apologists) the preexistent Christ exists in two stages. First, he exists in the mind of God from eternity. However, he is then begotten in time as a person. Thus his divinity is eternal, but his personhood is temporal. This is expounded upon in Wolfson, *Philosophy of the Church Fathers*, vol. 1.

*Methodology*

have been utilized heavily in Christian discussion from the early church onward, and are formative for later thought. These sources include three so-called apostolic fathers.[13] Clement of Rome, Ignatius of Antioch, and the anonymous *Epistle to Diognetus*, and the fourth is the earliest writer of extensive Christian treatises, Justin Martyr.

So why not the other apostolic fathers? Why not Polycarp, the *Didache*, Papias, 2 *Clement*, and *Barnabas*? Quite simply, they don't have much to say on the subject. Polycarp cites Ephesians 2:8 about salvation by grace rather than works,[14] then proceeds to exhort his readers to good works. Perhaps works are the result of this saving grace, or perhaps Polycarp views them as necessary for maintaining this salvation. The resurrection seems to be conditioned by the manner of one's life.[15] Polycarp does not explain whether works have a meritorious value or serve merely as vindication of the reality of faith. The evidence does not permit one to expand upon either of these statements to argue for a monergistic approach to salvation or justification through human merit. Thus, Polycarp is not particularly valuable in the present discussion.

The *Didache*, Papias, and Quadratus are so short as to be almost useless in this discussion. The *Didache* says nothing of law or justification.[16] Though it expands upon good works in some detail, the role of these works is left unknown. Whether they serve to maintain covenant status or are free works of faith is not expounded upon by this

---

13. The designation "apostolic fathers" is somewhat arbitrary, as *Diognetus* was likely written at the beginning of the period of the "apologists" rather than the end of the first/beginning of the second century as the other apostolic fathers.

14. Polycarp, *Phil.*, 1:3.

15. Ibid., 2:2.

16. At least not in a way relevant to the issue at hand.

short treatment of the moral life. Papias fragments are too small to be of any use,[17] as are those of Quadratus.

2 *Clement* is also unclear on the issue. Along with the fact that its author and dating remain unknown, his theology is also somewhat of a mystery. He opens his epistle proclaiming the mercies of God shown to him and his readers (and likely listeners), and the merits of the cross of Christ.[18] He then expands upon the necessity of works as confession of Christ before the world,[19] though sometimes Pseudo-Clement places a much higher value on works than simply confession of faith before men.[20] Perhaps a later study will establish the soteriology of 2 *Clement*, but I am left unsure of his thought in this area as is relevant to the discussion of justification and law.

*Barnabas* certainly has a plethora of things to say about the law, but most of these occur within his often bizarre spiritualizing exegesis of the Old Testament. Nothing is directly relevant to the discussion of the NPP and Luther's theology. He is thoroughly christological,[21] though the effects of Christ work are not made clear apart from the fact of its negating the old covenant law. He emphasizes good works, and may teach progressive justification through

---

17. Though Papias does expound, in a somewhat bizarre passage, about rewards in heaven based upon the merit of one's works, in Papias Fragment V.

18. *2 Clem.* 1:1—3:1.

19. This would not be inconsistent with a Lutheran approach to sanctification such as in Scaer, "Sanctification in Lutheran Theology," wherein Scaer proposes that sanctification is justification seen before men through good works done in love toward one's neighbor. Salvation is passive regarding God and active as seen by the world.

20. *2 Clem.* 6:7 for example.

21. *Barn.* 15:9 for example expounds upon the life of Christ, as he does throughout his epistle.

*Methodology*

works.[22] However, one statement made in passing is hardly enough to build an entire theology on.

Thus we are left with three significant figures in this discussion. Clement has a brief discussion of the doctrine of justification along with its relation to good works in the Christian life. *Diognetus* expounds upon the work of Christ thoroughly in its relation to righteousness, human sin, and eternal life. Ignatius does not contain a lengthy discussion on any of these issues, but the amount of material possessed by him far exceeds that of the other aforementioned apostolic fathers allows for a plausible reconstruction of his theology.

The earliest figure that may be seen as a glaring omission from this study is Irenaeus. Though writing somewhat later than Justin, Irenaeus provides one of the earliest in-depth theological accounts of early Christian doctrine. The reason Irenaeus has been left out of the study is the sheer amount of material he has written and scholarship associated with his soteriological views.[23] To address such a towering figure in a study such as this would not do justice to Irenaeus' thought. He merits a full-length study of his thought on these issues. Hopefully this will be done in the future, along with other major figures in the patristic era.

The edition of the apostolic fathers I have used is that of Michael W. Holmes, including his Greek text and English translations.[24] The classic Lightfoot translations were consulted as well, as they remain a valuable resource in patristic studies. For Justin's works, I have used the classic translations of the Schaff Ante-Nicene Fathers series.[25]

22. *Barn.* 4:10.

23. This is primarily to be found in Wingren, *Man and the Incarnation*, and subsequent articles dealing with Wingren's study which portrays a surprisingly "Lutheran" interpretation of Irenaeus.

24. *Apostolic Fathers*.

25. Justin, *Apostolic Fathers, Justin Martyr, Irenaeus. Justin,*

I have consulted modern translations as well, and used the Greek edition of G. Archambault from the early twentieth century.[26]

---

*Dialogue avec Tryphon.*
26. Justin, *Dialogue avec Tryphon*

# 3

# Previous Research on Patristic Soteriology

## THE REFORMATION

DISCUSSIONS OF JUSTIFICATION IN the early church are as old as the Reformation itself. For the Lutheran Reformation, it was imperative to establish not only the exegetical foundations for *sola fide*, but also to establish historical continuity with the early church. The first confession of the Reformation, the Augsburg Confession, defends the antiquity of *sola fide* with two authorities: Ambrose and Augustine.

> If anyone wants to be tricky and say that we have invented a new interpretation of Paul, this entire matter is supported by the testimony of the Fathers. Augustine defends grace and the righteousness of faith in many volumes against the merits of works. Ambrose, in his book *The*

> *Calling of the Gentiles*[1], and elsewhere, teaches the same thing. In *The Calling of the Gentiles* he says, "Redemption by Christ's blood would be worth very little, and God's mercy would not surpass man's works, if justification, which is accomplished through grace, were due to prior merits. So justification would not be the free gift from a donor but the reward due the laborer."[2]

The general consensus of the reformers was that there was a purer period in church history in which the righteousness of faith was taught correctly. During the Middle Ages, especially with the rise of Scholasticism, this teaching was lost. Aristotle had gained a foothold in the church and overshadowed Paul. Martin Luther did, however, find predecessors to his teachings in Bernard of Clairvaux, John Tauler, and the anonymous of author of the *Theologica Germanica*.

## GEORGE STANLEY FABER

The nineteenth century experienced a crisis in Anglican identity. Through the popularity of the Oxford movement, many Anglicans began reexamining the Protestant Reformation, adopting many of the teachings of the Roman Catholic Church. Those who adhered to the confessional identity of Anglicanism established in the Thirty-Nine Articles of Thomas Cranmer quickly responded in defense of the Reformation. George Stanley Faber was among these confessional Anglicans. Faber was primarily a patristic scholar, and while others argued on exegetical grounds, Faber wrote several books defending the antiquity of

---

1. This book is now generally regarded as the work of Prosper of Aquitaine, not Ambrose.

2. Augsburg, *Confessions*, art. 20.12–14, in McCain, *Concordia*.

## Previous Research on Patristic Soteriology

Protestant views on regeneration, election, Scripture, and justification.

In 1839, Faber published *The Primitive Doctrine of Justification Investigated*.[3] In this volume, Faber defends the thesis that the Protestant doctrine of *sola fide* is not a theological *novum*, but a reiteration of patristic teaching. This is important for Faber because "we turn to the unanimous consent of Primitive Antiquity for the best and surest *interpretation* of scripture: we are to receive no doctrine as an Article of Faith, save what *Scripture*, as interpreted by Antiquity, contains."[4] The fathers, for Faber, have a normative authority in biblical interpretation, thus an examination of patristic soteriology is necessary for a defense of *sola fide*.

Faber carries out his examination by selecting the most prominent fathers from the first four centuries, and subsequently writing quotes on the topic of justification. He writes on four apostolic fathers: Clement, Ignatius, the anonymous author of *the Epistle to Diognetus*, and Polycarp. In them, Faber finds what he understands as decisive evidence of *sola fide*. For Faber, all four of these authors clearly distinguish justification and sanctification in a reformational manner.

The early apologists of the Christian church also share a common understanding of justification, according to Faber. He insists that both Justin and Irenaeus explicitly teach forensic justification by faith. This extends to such varied writers as Clement of Alexandria, Cyprian, and even Origen. This treatment extends through the fourth century with Basil, Cyril of Jerusalem, Ambrose, Jerome, and Chrysostom. According to Faber, all of these writers teach a consistent Protestant gospel. He concludes with an analysis

---

3. Faber, Primitive Doctrine of Justification Investigated.
4. Ibid., xxxix.

of Augustine in which he defends the thesis that Augustine taught forensic justification.

Though Faber's work carries the advantage of studying writers individually, rather than compiling random quotes, his thesis ultimately fails. Faber begins his work with the presupposition that there *is* a unanimous consensus of the fathers. This forces him to defend the thesis that fathers such as Jerome and Clement of Alexandria taught Protestant distinctives, even though a casual reading of these sources would prove otherwise. Faber is less honest than many of the Reformers in his interpretation—hence, less convincing.

## THOMAS F. TORRANCE

In his doctoral dissertation, published as *The Doctrine of Grace in the Apostolic Fathers*,[5] Torrance argues that "The misunderstanding of the Gospel which took place as early as the second century, with the consequent relapse into non-Christian ideas, has resulted in a doctrine that is largely un-biblical."[6] This misunderstanding of the nature of the gospel was only partially remedied with the writings of Augustine and the Reformation.

Torrance attempts to prove his thesis through a thorough exegetical study of the apostolic fathers. He omits the *Epistle to Diognetus*, presumably because of its questionable dating. Torrance commences upon his study by analyzing the New Testament definition of grace. χαρις in the New Testament is connected with the unmerited love of God in Jesus Christ. This definition was largely abandoned in the second century through an adoption of the Hellenistic

---

5. Torrance, *Doctrine of Grace in the Apostolic Fathers*.
6. Ibid., v.

understanding of the term, separating grace from the person of Christ.

The *Didache* is examined first in Torrance's work. In this work of antiquity, Torrance claims that the Galatian error gains prominence over Paulinism. Rather than Paul's radical view that Christ saves apart from law, the *Didache* teaches that the error with Judaism is not salvation by the law *as such*, but in specific prescribed ordinances. For example, the *Didache* promotes prayer and fasting as meritorious acts, but prescribes different prayers and days of fasting than Judaism. The author fails to distinguish law and gospel by replacing Torah with a new law.

1 *Clement* fairs no better in Torrance's treatment. Torrance argues that conversions in the early church were not due to true faith in Christ, but a desire to live a virtuous life. The radical nature of the Christian gospel was replaced by a vague moralism. Clement is apparently a representative figure of this phenomenon. For Torrance, Clement's religion is based primarily in morality. Christ has no saving significance in himself, but is merely a teacher. Though Clement uses Pauline language, it is not used in a Pauline manner. In summary, God's grace is "only directed toward the pious."[7]

Torrance has a more positive evaluation of the epistles of Ignatius. In contrast to the other apostolic fathers, Ignatius' soteriology is thoroughly christological. Ignatius focuses on the incarnation, death, and resurrection of Christ in his soteric discussions. Ignatius, according to Torrance, still did not grasp the Pauline gospel; rather than forgiveness, which is the primary New Testament motif for salvation, Ignatius focuses on the estrangement between God and man which is overcome through the incarnation. He also ultimately views works as meritorious. Salvation is a matter of faith and love, not faith alone.

7. Ibid., 55.

Polycarp likewise is viewed by Torrance as christological, but without a full grasp of the Pauline gospel. Though he attributes salvation to grace, he views works as a requirement for the maintenance of the salvation achieved by Christ. Barnabas also is described as emphasizing the death and resurrection of Christ, but also falls into moralism. According to Torrance, Barnabas "knows nothing of the doctrine of a God who in sheer grace chooses the believer and justifies him."[8] Both Polycarp and Barnabas misunderstand the Pauline gospel.

Torrance's work is thorough, and is the most comprehensive available study on the soteriology of the earliest Christ writers. However, he is often too quick to dismiss statements in the fathers that might prove him wrong. For example, he dismisses Clement's discussion of justification apart from works without discussing the context of the quotation. He simply asserts that Clement does not use the language in a Pauline manner. His interpretation of the Pauline gospel is also a Barthian one, rather than a thoroughly reformational reading.[9] Any language of the necessity of perseverance is, for Torrance, evidence of works righteousness. This is not the case in a Lutheran reading.

## ALISTER MCGRATH

In the most comprehensive book ever written on the history of the doctrine of justification,[10] Alister McGrath writes a meager six pages on the pre-Augustinian patristic

8. Ibid., 106.

9. This is not a criticism, simply an observation of the theological presuppositions that differ in our studies. Barthian "objectivism" does not allow for any language of conditionality, even the language of faith.

10. McGrath, *Iustitia Dei*.

tradition. McGrath argues that Paulinism is not prevalent in the second-century church due to the prominence of the Gospels in Christian writings. He also argues that the lack of confrontation with Jewish Christians is a factor. The early Christians had other battles to fight; Judaism was not at the forefront. Thus the epistles of Romans and Galatians were not predominant.

According to McGrath, Justin Martyr emphasized human freedom and ability rather than God's grace. This came as a result of his previous philosophical training rather than theological deliberation. Justin's views were widely spread by Irenaeus and other early apologists in the fight against Gnosticism. In the fourth century, this emphasis was predominant in Chrysostom and Gregory of Nyssa.

The earliest Latin commentary on Romans was written by the writer known as Ambrosiaster. According to McGrath, Ambrosiaster did not view Paul as writing against a proto-Pelagian "salvation by works," but Jewish exclusivism. The law refers not to good works in general, but to ceremonial works. Ambrosiaster anticipates Pelagius in many ways, emphasizing the necessity of human merit for salvation. Similarly, Tertullian expounds human merit as a saving force.

McGrath's work in this time period is minimal. While he is correct about the prominence of Gnostic controversies and the Gospels in the early church, justification language is far from absent in the early church. Many fathers other than Ambrosiaster wrote Romans commentaries, such as Origen, Chrysostom, and Marius Victorinus. It is unfortunate that McGrath does not expound upon these and other writings.

The Righteousness of One

## THOMAS ODEN

The most extensive treatment of the topic of justification in the early church fathers in recent years has been Thomas Oden's *The Justification Reader*.[11] Oden proposes that there is a consensus among the fathers that justification comes by grace through faith. His motives are ecumenical as he seeks to move behind the reformation to a period in Christian history predating the East/West divide as well as the Protestant/Catholic divide. Though he claims many statements on the subject in the patristic sources are in accord with Roman Catholic and Eastern Orthodox teaching, he is bold enough to say, "I propose that this patristic teaching is profoundly in accord with strict Lutheran and Reformed teaching on justification, from Melancthon and Bucer to Gerhard and Owen to Hodge."[12] Oden commences upon this project by citing various church fathers on different aspects of the doctrine of justification including imputed righteousness, the nature of justifying faith, and the sufficiency of grace. He quotes such varied church fathers as Clement of Alexandria, Ambrose, Augustine, Origen, and Cyril of Jerusalem.

Oden's thesis proves unconvincing. Though admittedly this is only a reader geared toward laymen and scholar alike, it is still troubling that he fails to provide context for any of his citations. Many of these citations are interpreted by Oden in a Protestant manner; however, the writer he cites often merely uses the words "grace" and "faith" in a single thought. Often these writers are merely mimicking Paul's language without giving an interpretation of it, thus could be read in a way consistent with either Trent or the Augsburg Confession. Oden's proposal that there is

11. Oden, *Justification Reader*.
12. Ibid., 25.

*Previous Research on Patristic Soteriology*

an "orthodox consensus" at all in the first four centuries is highly debatable. There are few issues in which one would find agreement among such varied fathers as Jerome, Origen, Clement of Alexandria, Theodoret, Augustine, and Chrysostom. Even the nature of the Trinity and the nuances of the two natures of Christ have no unanimous approval by the fathers Oden chooses to cite. Much less would there be any consensus on an issue that was not at center stage in the theological battles of the day.

It is surprising that Oden can address such fathers as Origen and Jerome as teaching justification by faith alone apart from all of man's works when their reading of Paul's epistles to the Romans and Galatians interpret "works of the law" as Jewish works rather than man's works as such. This issue is not even addressed. Oden also seems to assume that justification for the fathers was not seen as a process indistinguishable from sanctification. He acknowledges this is an issue in most modern interpretations of Augustine but merely states that this is a wrong interpretation without giving a positive argument to the contrary.[13] The third clear omission from Oden's thesis is any discussion of *theosis*. He assumes that the term "righteousness" is used in a forensic rather than participationist categories in the fathers. This is not to say that a forensic reading of the fathers cannot exist simultaneously with some form of *theosis* in their thought. However, the issue at least needs to be addressed.

Oden's premise is admirable, and should be explored further. However, this must be done with an honest admission that there is a great diversity among the fathers on this issue. Protestant, Roman Catholic, and Orthodox alike can find traces of their soteriology in the fathers. However, each

13. Ibid., 20. He claims that he will provide an "overwhelming presentation of evidence to the contrary" later in the volume, but fails to do so.

tradition has taken strands of teaching from various fathers. For example, Jerome's interpretation of "works of the law" has been particularly influential in the development of Roman Catholic theology, whereas Augustine's interpretation of this phrase would play a crucial role in Luther's reading of Paul's anti-Judaizing polemic. Each father needs to be studied individually, and the subject of justification placed in their overall theological framework.

## NICK NEEDHAM

In an essay titled "Justification in the Early Church Fathers,"[14] Nick Needham defends the thesis that there are strands of a Protestant understanding of justification in the pre-Augustinian church. Needham does not pretend that there is a consensus of teaching among the fathers, admitting that there is no "single coherent monolith"[15] within the teachings of the patristic writers. Even individual authors are not consistent in their own language and teachings.

According to Needham, the fathers often taught a forensic understanding of the term "justification." Chrysostom specifically places justification within a law court setting while defining the term in his Romans commentary.[16] Several patristic writers contrast justification with condemnation. This shows that justification functions as language of acquittal.

Furthering his argument, Needham attempts to demonstrate that imputed righteousness is a prevalent concept in numerous fathers. He continues with quotations from Justin Martyr, Irenaeus, Ambrosiaster, and Chrysostom.

14. Needham, "Justification in the Early Church Fathers."
15. Ibid., 27.
16. Chrysostom's comments on Rom 3:4b.

*Previous Research on Patristic Soteriology*

For Needham, this merits the conclusion that "We have, then, in the fathers of the first four centuries, this major strand of justification teaching where the meaning is forensic: a not-guilty verdict, an acquittal, a declaration of righteousness, a nonimputation of sins, an imputation of righteousness."[17] Hence, the Reformation teaching on justification stands squarely on patristic ground.

Though Needham convincingly demonstrates that justification is often used in a legal context in early Christian writings, his conclusion is premature. He fails to address how Justin Martyr can teach imputed righteousness in a reformational manner, while simultaneously declaring that "each one ... shall be saved by his own righteousness."[18] Needham quotes Irenaeus without relating his view of justification to his concept of recapitulation, which appears as the overriding soteriological motif in his writings. Though Needham is careful to allow for discrepancy and other views within the early church, he still fails to provide context for his quotations, or their place within the overall thought of each figure.

The second part of Needham's essay is more convincing and honest than what precedes it. Needham argues that when speaking of conversion, the fathers teach justification by faith alone. However, works have prominence in the Christian life, as maintenance for salvation. For example, Chrysostom can write about almsgiving as a saving force. However, Needham points out that almsgiving is viewed as a channel of God's mercy and continual forgiveness rather than a strict act of merit.

Needham's essay is helpful in its honesty. He admits discrepancies, and allows for penance, as well as the essential nature of baptism, in one's salvation. However, it lacks

17. Needham, "Justification in the Early Church Fathers," 36.
18. Justin, *Dialogue with Trypho*, sec. 45.

the convincing power of a full examination of the view of select fathers, by writing a fuller treatment. This, however, is beyond the scope of an article.

## D. H. WILLIAMS

In perhaps the most effective and convincing meditation on the subject,[19] D. H. Williams argues that there is precedence for a view of *sola fide* in certain church fathers. Williams correctly observes that "The teaching of justification prior to Augustine seems to be largely ignored by doctrinal historians."[20] He criticizes McGrath's unfortunate negligence of the first four centuries in his monumental study of the doctrine of justification, as well as T. F. Torrance's dismissal of the apostolic fathers as proponents of works righteousness.

Williams focuses primarily on Hilary of Poitier's view of justification in his Matthew commentary. However, before doing so, Williams briefly discusses the status of the doctrine within the first three centuries of church history. He shows how Polycarp begins his letter with the Pauline theme of justification by grace. This also is apparent in Clement's epistle to the Corinthians and the anonymous *Epistle to Diognetus*. Williams admits that other early works such as the *Didache* and the *Shepherd of Hermas* show a differing view of salvation, in which works have a prominent role.

Williams then briefly discusses the works of Origen and Marius Victorinus. He argues that while Origen sometimes speaks of an initial justification by faith alone, he allows faith and works to coincide as a saving unity.

19. Williams, "Justification by Faith."
20. Ibid., 651.

*Previous Research on Patristic Soteriology*

Victorinus, on the other hand, discusses justification by faith alone but writes an insignificant amount for one to determine his precise meaning.

Williams demonstrates that Hilary views justification as a central element of Christian proclamation. This is apparent in the fact that Hilary uses the term *fides iustificat* twenty times in a commentary on Matthew (significantly, not a work of Paul). Hilary consistently contrasts faith and works. The pharisaical way of life demanded salvation by merit, however, the Christian is saved by his faith. Hilary even expressly uses the phrase *fides sola iustificat*. Williams concludes that "Theological skepticism about the priority of saving faith and unmerited grace in the pre-Augustinian period has been overstated."[21]

William's article proves the most convincing work on the subject. He admits that not all fathers agree, citing the specific examples of *Hermas* and the *Didache*. While many other works acknowledge differing views, they often proceed as if a unanimous consensus of the fathers still exists. Williams also has the benefit of focusing on one specific figure, rather than summing up the entire pre-Augustinian church within a single article.

---

21. Ibid., 666.

# 4

# Which Luther?

## An Assessment of Luther's Pauline Interpretation

CENTRAL TO KRISTER STENDAHL's thesis that asserts that Paul has been misread through Lutheran interpretation is a reading of Luther that assumes continuity between Luther and the Lutheran scholastic tradition.[1] This continuity has been assumed to have resulted in the twentieth-century Bultmannian reading of Paul, whose chief concern is man's individual existential plight.[2] It is my contention that this is a fundamental misunderstanding of Luther's (and the early Lutheran tradition for that matter) explication of the

1. This is not to imply that the portrayal of the scholastic tradition is entirely accurate either. Scholasticism is a much richer tradition than is often realized.

2. For Bultmann's understanding of the issue see Bultmann, *Theology of the New Testament*; MacQuarrie, *Existentialist Theology*; or Young, *History and Existential Theology*.

*Which Luther?*

doctrine of justification. Luther is not the individualist he is often painted as, nor is Luther concerned with an emphatically legal interpretation of justification to the detriment of all of the varied New Testament motifs for salvation.

For centuries the standard reading of Luther assumed that he interpreted Paul as an opponent of Jewish legalism who opposed justification by works with the concept of a legal imputation of the believer's sin to Christ and of Christ's righteousness to the believer. The scholastic categories of seventeenth-century Lutheranism were believed to have been taken from the thought of the great reformer himself; however, within the past few decades this reading has been challenged.

In the mid-1970s a group of Finnish scholars, led by Tuomo Mannermaa, began to reevaluate Luther's understanding of justification in the midst of an ecumenical dialogue between the Lutheran Church of Finland and the Russian Orthodox Church. Seeking to find common ground among the two theological traditions, the doctrine of *theosis* became a central point of discussion, especially in relation to the theology of Luther. Maannerma's influential work, *Christ Present in Faith*,[3] argues that Luther's view of justification was not one of mere imputation; this was an innovation of Luther's disciple Melanchthon. For Luther, justification includes an indwelling of the person of Christ. Christ is not outside of the believer in a law court, placing his works before the Father to satisfy the demands of divine justice. Christ, as the righteous God-man, imputes his righteousness through divine indwelling.

As the title suggests, Mannermaa shows that Luther believed that Christ's person is present within the believer's faith. It can even be said that Christ *is* faith. Faith has usually been seen in Lutheran dogmatics as a gift created by

3. Mannermaa, *Christ Present in Faith*.

the Spirit in the heart of the believer. However, for Luther, it is an uncreated grace because it is the presence of Christ himself. Mannermaa argues that the research of the Luther renaissance has been overly influenced by neo-Kantian epistemology and ontology. Albrecht Ritschl's influential Luther study[4] attempted to show that Luther held to an epistemology similar to that of Hermann Lotze. In this framework, there is no being-in-itself that can be known. A thing can only be known by its effects upon a subject. Thus, when Ritschl read Luther's statements of Christ being "present in faith," he interpreted this as an external impulse of God that affects the human will. His being "with us" or "in us" is a way of stating that the believer lives in and for Christ. There is no ontological union between the believer and Christ; rather, there is a unity of will and action.

Even a cursory reading of Luther demonstrates that Luther held to the philosophical framework of his times. What a man perceives through his senses and reasons through his intellect corresponds to an object in reality, not merely a thing's effects. Thus, for Luther, man's encounter with God includes participation in God's being, not merely his influence or will. Mannermaa writes, "[W]hat God gives of himself to humans is nothing separate from God himself."[5] This union of being between God in man results in man's divinization, so that Luther can repeat without hesitation the famous Athanasian dictum that God became man so that man may become god.

Though this new move in Luther scholarship may take issue with the interpretations of Luther in the Lutheran confessional documents,[6] they are not willing to throw

---

4. An insightful take on Ritsch's interpretation of Luther can be found in Lotz, *Ritschl & Luther*.

5. Mannermaa, "Why Is Luther so Fascinating?," 10.

6. Mannermaa quite freely disagrees with the Formula of

*Which Luther?*

out categories like "imputation" and "alien righteousness," which have been at the heart of the Lutheran theological tradition since the sixteenth century. The righteousness that belongs to the believer is that of Christ and not that of his own. In this way, it can be said that it is "alien." However, it is not "outside of us" in the sense that it is a bare declaration of righteousness upon one who is unrighteous.[7] It includes the external disposition of God *and* an internal presence of the Trinity. Christ comes as both grace *and* gift: "Christ himself, both his person and his work, is the ground of Christian righteousness."[8] Salvation, for Luther, is a two-sided coin: on the one hand God's wrath is propitiated and he now has a gracious disposition toward the believer, and on the other God himself is present within the believer.

Mannermaa argues that this view of Luther identifies him more closely with the thought of the early church. It may be said that Luther's view of justification came largely through "Chalcedonian" considerations. Luther is able to talk about Christ as the "greatest sinner" not only in the sense that sins were imputed to him, but because Christ took upon himself a real human nature. Christ participates in sinful humanity in a realistic way. In the same manner, the believer participates in Christ, thus receiving Christ's very righteousness. There is something of a *communicatio idiomatum* between Christ and the believer. This results in the believer and Christ becoming one person. "In faith, the

---

Concord at several points, for instance: "In Luther's theology, however, the relation between justification and the divine indwelling in the believer is, undoubtedly, defined differently from the formulation of the Formula of Concord" (*Union With Christ*, 28). As I will demonstrate later, such contradiction does not necessarily exist.

7. This is not an acceptance of Osiander's view, which defines righteousness as an attribute of the divine nature alone.

8. Mannermaa, "Justification and *Theosis* in Lutheran-Orthodox Perspective," 10.

person of Christ and that of the believer are made one, and this oneness must not be divided."⁹

One may be tempted to discard Mannermaa's interpretation as being formulated merely to defend an ecumenical agenda without a careful reading of the texts. After all, it is difficult to defend the thesis that so many centuries of Luther scholarship have been wrong on this central point. Have most readings of Luther been based upon the assumption that there is agreement between Luther and the later confessional documents of the Book of Concord? More so, have Kantian presuppositions shaped so much of Lutheran theological thinking and missed Luther's own epistemic assumptions? Only a look at Luther's texts themselves can answer this question.

## THE EARLY LUTHER

## Two Kinds of Righteousness

The work in which the early reformation Luther is most explicit in his views on justification is his late 1518 or early 1519 sermon on the *Two Kinds of Righteousness*. The first kind of righteousness, as Luther describes it, is an alien righteousness. The second is that which grows out of faith in love to our neighbor. This first kind of righteousness is properly that of Christ, not the believer. However, the believer is given to share in this righteousness. He uses the imagery of a bride and her groom: "Just as a bridegroom possesses all that is the bride's and she all that is his- for the two have all things in common because they are one flesh . . . so Christ and the church are one spirit."¹⁰ Luther

9. Mannermaa, *Christ Present in Faith*, 42.
10. Luther, *Luther's Works* (hereafter *LW*), 31:297.

*Which Luther?*

is drawing upon the common theme of his mystical heritage that the believer's soul is united to and participates in the being of God. He, unlike many of his forbearers, prefers the image of the church over that of the individual. Also in agreement with the medieval tradition, Luther sees the gifts of Christ as being given through baptism and repentance.[11] Through faith, the believer is not only given Christ's benefits, but also Christ himself: "Through faith in Christ, therefore, Christ's righteousness becomes our righteousness and all the he has becomes ours; rather, he himself becomes ours."[12] As Mannermaa explains, "Christ is both the *favor* and the *donum*."[13] Luther does not connect Christ's righteousness to his active obedience to the law. Throughout this sermon, legal metaphors of salvation are far from dominant. He expresses his thoughts primarily with participationist language. Rather than righteousness being imputed over the believer's own sin, Luther describes this righteousness as that which is "an infinite righteousness, one that swallows up all sins in a moment, for it is impossible that sin should exist in Christ; [the Christian] is one with Christ, having the same righteousness as he."[14] The believer is not condemned because he participates in Christ's person.[15] As one who is divine, Christ does not and cannot sin. Thus, through the Christian's participation in divinity, sin is not imputed to him. Luther sees Christ's righteousness not merely as a legal covering, but as that which effects sanctification:

11. "This righteousness, then, is given to men in baptism and whenever they truly repent" (Ibid.).

12. Ibid., 298.

13. Mannermaa, *Christ Present in Faith*, 5.

14. *LW* 31:298.

15. Mannermaa is right in saying that for Luther, "justifying faith does not merely signify a reception of the forgiveness imputed to a human being for the sake of the merit of Christ, which is the aspect emphasized by the *Formula of Concord*" (*Christ Present in Faith*, 17).

## The Righteousness of One

"Christ daily drives out the old Adam more and more in accordance with the extent to which faith and knowledge of Christ grow. For alien righteousness is not instilled all at once, but it begins, makes progress, and is finally perfected at the end through death."[16] The believer is gradually perfected in his union with Christ until his Adamic nature is no longer present. Luther sees justification as a progressive act of participation in divinity, not merely an instantaneous forensic reality.

The second part of Luther's sermon describes the Christian's life of obedience. This is said to be the righteousness properly belonging to the believer. It is not however, a separate benefit from Christ's righteousness, but is the result of it. As Christ's presence grows in the believer, his Adamic nature dies and he begins to freely love his neighbor. Luther again returns to the metaphor of marriage: the bridegroom, Christ, claims the believer as his own. This he does through giving his own righteousness freely to his beloved, granting assurance of forgiveness and salvation. In return, the soul reaches out to others in love without self interest: "Then the soul no longer seeks to be righteous in and for itself, but has Christ as its righteousness and therefore seeks only the welfare of others."[17] The Christian life is grounded on the indwelling Christ.

The assumption can easily be made, with scholastic distinctions in mind, that the first kind of righteousness that Luther describes is justification, and the second is sanctification. However, it is more accurate to understand the first kind of righteousness as containing both aspects of salvation. Neither justification nor sanctification is the work of man; both are wholly monergistic acts and the result of alien righteousness. Mannermaa correctly explains Luther's view of

16. Ibid., 299.
17. *LW* 31:300.

## Which Luther?

sanctification: "Christ is, thus, the true agent of good works in the Christian."[18] The second kind of righteousness Luther describes is merely the outward actions that display the sanctifying work of Christ within him.[19]

## On Christian Liberty

Of Luther's three famous Reformation treatises written in 1520, *On Christian Liberty* most directly addresses the issue at hand. Luther here sets out to write a popular devotional book based upon his newly discovered doctrine of justification by faith. Though not a treatise written directly on the topic of justification, Luther writes more about the subject in this small volume than in any other of his early works. Thus, this is the most important work of the young Luther for the present study.

Addressing the issue of Paul's spirit and flesh dualism, Luther argues in surprisingly Platonic terms:[20] "According to the spiritual nature, which men refer to as the soul, [the Christian] is called a spiritual, inner or new man. According to the bodily nature, which men refer to as flesh, he is called a carnal, outward, or old man."[21] Works such as fasting and pilgrimages cannot contribute to a man's spiritual well being because these things affect the bodily aspect of man, rather than the seat of spirituality, the soul. However,

18. Mannermaa, *Christ Present in Faith*, 50.

19. There is no distinction between "getting in" and "staying in" for Luther. Both are acts of pure grace and are benefits received through faith. Any kind of "covenantal nomism" would be, for Luther, merely another form of works righteousness.

20. This strict body/soul or physical/spiritual dichotomy is not found in the later Luther. Especially in the sacramental controversies Luther adopts a much more holistic ontology.

21. *LW* 31:344.

righteousness and freedom have an influence over the soul, thus these are proper to Christian salvation.

Through faith in Christ, the believer is spiritually resurrected, forgiven, and imputed righteous by the merit of Christ. The Word indwells the Christian and "the soul is justified, by the word of God, sanctified, made true, peaceful, and free, filled with every blessing and made a child of God."[22] Luther likens the union between Christ and the soul to heat and iron. When fire touches an iron, the iron though not being transformed into fire, exhibits many of the qualities of fire. In the same way, the Word imparts his qualities to the soul in union with him. This is the same metaphor used by several church fathers and later Lutheran dogmaticians to describe the relation between Christ's human and divine natures. Mannermaa is justified in referring to this as a *communicatio idiomatum* between Christ and the believer. For Luther, an understanding of the two natures in Christ is necessary for understanding salvation.

Luther again returns to the analogy of the bridegroom and the bride. Like many in the mystical tradition before him, Luther teaches that "Christ and the soul become one flesh."[23] The soul, being full of sin and wickedness, is given to Christ, thus Christ is counted as sinful and wicked. On the other hand, the soul is counted as righteous, just and holy through sharing the attributes of the bridegroom. Luther still does not use legal language referring to imputation and forgiveness, but speaks of our sins being "swallowed" by Christ's righteousness. This is not the righteousness of his divinity alone, but of his sinless human life. Once again, in agreement with Mannermaa, the language of participation in the divine is dominant.

22. *LW* 31:349.
23. *LW* 31:351.

*Which Luther?*

Faith does not only allow the Christian to be forgiven but also cleanses the soul and the believer is "made to love God."[24] It also causes the believer to be "restored to Paradise and created anew."[25] Using the image of a tree and its fruit, Luther argues that faith creates man anew, and works flow from his new nature. To argue that one must do works to make himself a Christian would be tantamount to telling someone to make peaches so that they may become a peach tree. Luther has not made the later divide between justification and regeneration, as he sees justification as that which creates the new man.

## Summary

It has been sufficiently shown that the early Luther teaches that justification involves an ontological connection between the believer and Christ. The believer is sinful, and Christ righteous. Because Christ's righteousness is infinitely greater than the believer's sin, the believer is forgiven and considered righteous through this union. Justification is something that grows in the believer, killing the old Adam. This righteousness seals the marriage relationship between Christ and the soul, allowing the believer to exist as one who lives in selfless love toward his neighbor.

### 1535 GALATIANS COMMENTARY

Mannermaa's study is based primarily on the work of the late Luther and his monumental study on Galatians. Whether one agrees with Luther's reading of Paul or not, it must be admitted that this work deserves its reputation as a

24. *LW* 31:359.
25. *LW* 31:360.

theological masterpiece. Much more than a basic outline of Luther's law and gospel distinction, this commentary weaves together nearly all of the themes of Luther's theology and comments on Paul's original words. Similar to Barth's 1919 Romans commentary,[26] Luther's work is more of a theological manifesto than a carefully studied work of exegesis.

Beginning his commentary, Luther describes Christian righteousness as

> . . . the righteousness of faith, which God imputes to us through Christ without works, [it] is neither political nor ceremonial nor legal nor work-righteousness, but is quite the opposite; it is a merely passive righteousness, while all the others, listed above, are active. For here we work nothing, render nothing to God; we only receive and permit someone else to work in us, namely, God.[27]

This definition sets the tone for the rest of the work as Luther is primarily arguing a case for passive righteousness over the active righteousness of the "formed faith" described in late scholasticism. Luther describes this passive righteousness as that which is the work of God "in us."

## Defining Justification

The first question to be addressed, to which the answer has so often been assumed, is what the later Luther means by the use of the term justification. Post-Reformation Lutheran orthodoxy would define justification by distinguishing its two aspects: the forgiveness of sins and the imputation of righteousness.[28] A further distinction is made between

---

26. Barth, *Epistle to the Romans*.

27. *LW* 26:4–5.

28. For example, "Thus according to Scripture we have a twofold

the passive and active obedience of Christ. Christ's passive obedience includes his life-giving death, paying the penalty of the law on behalf of sinners; his active obedience includes his sinless life, being perfectly obedient to the law. Through faith this obedience is put to the Christian's account.

Many Luther scholars assume that these distinctions exist, at least in seed form, in the writings of Luther himself. Saarnivaara can assert: "Luther teaches that man must first be justified and possess by faith the perfect fulfillment of the law accomplished by Christ."[29] Saarnivaara says this after quoting numerous statements by Luther that refer to justification by the merits of Christ. However, none of the quotations cited make mention of Christ's active obedience to the law. It has so often been taken for granted that the later tradition accurately represented Luther that upon reading the words "righteousness of Christ" one assumes the definition of "active obedience to the law." However, in his Galatians commentary, perhaps Luther's most extensive work on the topic, Luther makes no mention to Christ's active obedience to the law. He connects the righteousness of Christ to his divine righteousness, his death, his resurrection, and even his human sinlessness, but never to his perfect law keeping. Though he occasionally makes statements of Christ being put under the law for us, there are insufficient grounds for assuming a later scholastic doctrine in Luther. Saarnivaara and others fail to show that Luther held to the active obedience of Christ as a necessary aspect of the Christian's justification.

---

term for the essence of justification- first a negative term, namely, the nonimputation of sins, and second a positive term, namely, the imputation of Jesus' righteousness" (Hoenecke, *Evangelical Lutheran Dogmatics*, 3:330).

29. Saarnivaara, *Luther Discovers the Gospel*, 16.

## The Righteousness of One

McGrath approaches Luther from a very different perspective: "Luther did not teach a doctrine of forensic justification in the strict sense. The concept of forensic justification necessitates a deliberate and systematic distinction between justification and regeneration, a distinction which is not found in Luther's earlier works."[30] For McGrath, Luther did not depart from the Augustinian tradition in viewing justification as a process. He did differ however in seeing justification wholly as the result of the righteousness of Christ devoid of human cooperation.

It is clear that McGrath is right about Luther's early writings. Luther can speak of "growing in alien righteousness" as well as being "partly righteous" and "partly sinful" in the context of justification. Luther uses similar language in his 1535 Galatians commentary, though less often than the young Luther: "There is a double life: my own, which is natural or animate; and an alien life, that of Christ in me. So far as my animate life is concerned, I am dead and am now living an alien life."[31] Alien righteousness does not include merely imputation, but also the gradual growth in holiness brought about by the power of Christ. "However, Luther more commonly refers to justification as an event, rather than a process, especially related to the beginning of the Christian life.[32] For Luther, justification is an event, brought about by faith alone, wherein one receives forgiveness and the alien righteousness of Christ." For Luther, justification is the beginning of the Christian life, brought about by faith alone in the alien righteousness of Christ. Alien righteousness also effects sanctification so that both the declaration and progression in righteousness are extra nos. Imputation

---

30. McGrath, "Forerunners of the Reformation?," 225.

31. *LW* 26:170.

32. For example, "But once we have been justified by faith, we enter the active life" (*LW* 26:287).

*Which Luther?*

and renewal are so connected that Luther is comfortable at times using progressive language in reference to justification. One's sanctification is, in a sense, bringing about the reality of the past event of justification.

McGrath is correct, however, in saying that in Luther the distinction between justification and regeneration is not yet made. In his so called "last will and testament," the Smalcald Articles, Luther gives a clear statement about the meaning of justification: "I do not know how to change in the least what I have previously and constantly taught about justification. Namely, that through faith we have a new and clean heart, and God will and does account us entirely righteous and holy for the sake of Christ our Mediator."[33] Even at the end of his life, Luther is content to subsume both the initial change of heart and imputation under the term "justification." This is why Luther so often uses the analogy of the tree and its fruit.[34]

For the late Luther of the 1535 Galatians commentary, justification is an instantaneous event, not a process. It includes the imputation of righteousness, forgiveness of sins, and the renewal of the heart. This all occurs through Christ's alien righteousness which then affects sanctification, not as distinct from, but as the fulfillment of justification. McGrath correctly reads early Luther, but misses Luther's later more nuanced position that justification is instantaneous but its fulfillment is progressive.

---

33. Smalcald Articles 3.13.1, in McCain, *Concordia*.

34. "Thus he is a true doer of the Law who receives the Holy Spirit through faith in Christ and then begins to love God and to do good to his neighbor. Hence "to do" includes faith at the same time. Faith takes the doer himself and makes him into a tree, and his deeds become fruit. First there must be a tree, then the fruit" (*LW* 26:255).

## The Righteousness of One

### Deification

With the context of Luther's meaning of the term "justification" in mind, Mannermaa's thesis that the soteriology for the late Luther includes participation in divinity, may be sufficiently dealt with. Mannermaa's key text for interpretation in Luther's Galatians commentary is as follows:

> Such are the dreams of the scholastics. But where they speak of love, we speak of faith. And while they say that faith is the mere outline but love is its living colors and completion, we say in opposition that faith takes hold of Christ and that He is the form that adorns and informs faith as color does the wall. Therefore Christian faith is not an idle quality or an empty husk in the heart, which may exist in a state of mortal sin until love comes along and makes it alive. But if it is true faith, it is a sure trust and firm acceptance in the heart. It takes hold of Christ in such a way that Christ is the object of faith, or rather not the object but, so to speak, the One who is present in the faith itself. Thus faith is a sort of knowledge or darkness that nothing can see. Yet the Christ of whom faith takes hold is sitting in this darkness as God sat in the midst of darkness on Sinai and in the temple. Therefore our "formal righteousness" is not a love that informs faith; but it is faith itself, a cloud in our hearts, that is, trust in a thing we do not see, in Christ, who is present especially when He cannot be seen.[35]

In light of the evidence in Luther's early writings, Mannermaa's interpretation is the only plausible one. There is no language of a moral influence in this text; neither is there language of a law court. Unless Luther gives us sufficient

---

35. *LW* 26:129.

*Which Luther?*

reason to think otherwise, it must be assumed that the language he uses in his early writings carries a similar meaning here. Thus the most obvious interpretation is that faith holds on to Christ. It does not only receive his benefits but grasps his person.

This interpretation is further supported by the picture Luther draws in his imagery of a ring that grasps a jewel: "Faith takes hold of Christ and has Him present, enclosing Him as the ring encloses the gem. And whoever is found having this faith in the Christ who is grasped in the heart, him God accounts as righteous."[36] As the ring is not merely imputed as having qualities of a diamond, the believer is not merely counted as having the righteousness of another. Faith grasps Christ who comes into the believer's heart. Through the indwelling of the person of Christ, the believer has the infinite righteousness of Christ inside of him and, consequently, is imputed as righteous before the Father. This righteousness is of Christ's humanity and divinity, and is tied to the incarnation, cross, and resurrection through the reception of Christ in faith.

There is an assumed ontology in Luther that one shares in the being of his object of faith. Luther writes that "Works or love are not the ornament or perfection of faith; but faith itself is a gift of God, a work of God in our hearts, which justifies us because it takes hold of Christ as the Savior. Human reason has the law as its object. It says to itself: 'This I have done; this I have not done.' But faith in its proper function has no other object than Christ."[37] If one has faith in the law, he participates in the law as his life and misses Christ. In the scholastic portrayal of "faith formed by love" one has love as his object. Luther fought so vehemently against this phrase, not because he did not believe that faith must be

36. *LW* 26:132.
37. *LW* 26:88.

active in love, but because it formulated love as the object of one's faith, rather than Christ. One cannot be saved by participating in love, but participating in Christ.[38]

Mannermaa argues that Luther's view of the believer's union with Christ comes from Chalcedonian considerations. As seen in his earlier works, Luther continues to use christological analogies to refer to the union between the believer and Christ. As in the person of Christ human nature and divine nature are joined together in one person without mixture, confusion, or separation, it may be said that the believer and Christ become one person: "But here Christ and my conscience must become one body, so that nothing remains in my sight but Christ, crucified and risen."[39] Luther still feels content to liken this union to the analogy of a bride and bridegroom. However, by this time Luther shed much of his Platonic orientation, and his language has became more holistic. It is the whole man who is united with Christ rather than merely the soul. Luther places the reception of salvation within this context:

> But so far as justification is concerned, Christ and I must be so closely attached that He lives in me and I in Him. What a marvelous way of speaking! Because He lives in me, whatever grace, righteousness, life, peace, and salvation there is in me is all Christ's; nevertheless, it is mine as well, by the cementing and attachment that are through faith, by which we become as one body in the Spirit.[40]

Luther goes so far as to say that without this ontological union one could not be saved: "When it comes to

---

38. For a more in-depth discussion of Luther's ontology, see Juntunen, "Luther and Metaphysics."

39. *LW* 26:166.

40. *LW* 26:167–68.

## Which Luther?

justification, therefore, if you divide Christ's Person from your own, you are in the Law; you remain in it and live in yourself, which means that you are dead in the sight of God and damned by the Law."[41] The union of persons is not a subsidiary doctrine, but is essential to Luther's understanding of salvation.

Luther does not only use Chalcedonian concepts to describe the participation of being between man and Christ, but in Christ himself as he comes to dwell with and save his people. Both Christ's divine nature and human nature are vital for Christian salvation. Luther often connects the divinity of Christ with his ability to conquer death and save: "Now since Christ has conquered the Law in His own Person, it necessarily follows that He is God by nature."[42] For Christ's righteousness to save, it must be an infinite righteousness, which could only be the righteousness of God himself.

However, unlike Osiander, Luther does not see the indwelling righteousness of divinity as capable of saving.[43] Humans need a savior who is also a man, or perhaps more accurately, one who takes upon himself not just the nature of one individual man, but of humanity itself. When the Christian is in despair over the state of his soul, Luther admonishes one to look to God hidden in this man: "Therefore whenever you consider the doctrine of justification and wonder how or where or in what condition to find a God who justifies or accepts sinners, then you must know that there is no other God than this Man Jesus Christ."[44] The doctrine of justification flows out of the truth of the

41. *LW* 26:36.

42. *LW* 26:36.

43. For a balanced approach to Osiander's theology, see Wilson-Kastner, "Andreas Osiander's Theology of Grace."

44. *LW* 26:29.

Chalcedonian creed. He must be fully God so that he has the power to save and rise from the dead. He must be fully man so that he can truly take the curse due to humanity. "Thus He joined God and man in one Person. And being joined with us who were accursed, He became a curse for us; and He concealed His blessing in our sin, death, and curse, which condemned and killed Him. But because He was the Son of God, He could not be held by them."[45] The doctrine of Christ's two natures is the groundwork for the doctrine of justification.

## Luther and Eschatology

One aspect of Luther's understanding of justification comes out clearly in the Galatians commentary but is often ignored in many treatments of Luther, including that of Mannermaa: his focus on eschatology. Rather than connecting righteousness to Christ's sinless life under the law, Luther connects Christ's righteousness with his resurrection.[46] Commenting on Galatians 1:1, Luther states:

> The addition of these words, "and through God the Father, etc.," seems to be superfluous. But because, as I have said, he is speaking from the abundance of his heart, his mind is aflame with the yearning to express, even at the very beginning of his epistle, the unsearchable riches of Christ (Eph 3:8) and to preach the righteousness of God which is called the resurrection of the dead. Christ, who lives and has been raised from

---

45. *LW* 26:290.

46. This idea of resurrection as connected with justification has seen resurgence within Pauline interpretation as well. Reformed scholar Richard B. Gaffin Jr. has made this point in *Resurrection and Redemption*.

*Which Luther?*

the dead, is speaking though him and prompting him to speak this way. Therefore he calls God "the Father, who raised Jesus Christ from the dead." It is as though he were to say: "I have to contend with Satan and with those vipers, Satan's instruments, who are trying to rob me of the righteousness of Christ, who was raised from the dead by God the Father. By this righteousness alone we are justified, and by it we shall also be raised from death to eternal life on the Last Day. But those who are trying to undermine the righteousness of Christ are resisting the Father as well as the Son and the work of both of Them."

Thus at the very outset Paul explodes with the entire issue he intends to set forth in this epistle. He refers to the resurrection of Christ, who rose again for our justification (Rom 4:25). His victory is a victory over the Law, sin, our flesh, the world, the devil, death, hell, an all evils; and this victory of His He has given to us. Even though these tyrants, our enemies, accuse us and terrify us, they cannot drive us into despair or condemn us. For Christ, whom God the Father raised from the dead, is the Victor over them, and He is our righteousness. Therefore "thanks be to God, who has given us the victory through our Lord Jesus Christ" (1 Cor 15:57). Amen.[47]

Luther defines God's righteousness as the vindication of Christ at his resurrection. Contrary to the neglect of resurrection theology in many later Lutheran theologians,[48] Luther is content to define the whole gospel by the resurrection of Christ. It is the "entire issue" Paul is arguing for

---

47. *LW* 26:9.

48. Pieper, for example, has barely over two pages on the resurrection under the discussion of the states of Christ. See Pieper, *Christian Dogmatics*, 2:320–23.

in the central book of the New Testament. This is not a mere spiritual resurrection to comfort the individual conscience, but a physical resurrection from the dead that will result in the physical resurrection of Christ's people on the Last Day.

The central place for resurrection in Luther's theology is not only present in the later Luther but permeates all of his writings. In his 1519 Galatians lectures, Luther argues that denial of the resurrection necessarily leads to justification by works. The converse is also true: "For those who maintain that righteousness comes by works deny Christ's resurrection and even ridicule it."[49] Through belief in Christ's resurrection the believer "also rises and lives in Christ, and Christ live in him."[50] Christ's resurrection is not only the basis for spiritual regeneration but also secures physical resurrection. Luther does not see the resurrection as something that teaches a moral lesson, nor does he see it as proof of Christ's divinity, or a mere declaration that the propitiation on the cross was sufficient. The resurrection itself effects salvation.[51]

For Luther, as for Paul, salvation involves past, present, and future blessings. Though the old Adam will only die at one's death, and the resurrection will only occur at Christ's return, the believer participates presently, through faith and the sacraments, in the eschatological kingdom of God. Luther says of justification, "When I have this righteousness within me, I descend from heaven like the rain that makes the earth fertile. That is, I come forth into another kingdom, and I perform good works whenever the opportunity

---

49. *LW* 27:167–68.

50. *LW* 27:167–68.

51. Perhaps this theme of resurrection is the common ground to be found amongst Eastern Orthodox and Lutheran soteriology, which ecumenical dialogues have been searching for.

arises."[52] Justification is more than a legal declaration; it brings the believer out of the kingdom of Satan and into the kingdom of God. Justification is an eschatological verdict based on union with the resurrected Christ.

## ASSESSMENT OF MANNERMAA'S THESIS

Mannermaa's contention that there is an ontological aspect to salvation in the theology of Luther is correct. Salvation includes the imputation of righteousness and the forgiveness of sins, but none of these benefits can be given without an ontological union between the believer and Christ. The early Luther argues primarily in participationist categories, seeing the righteousness of God as the infinite righteousness of divinity, along with the resurrection, which the believer participates in so that he may be accepted, forgiven, and gradually made holy. The later Luther argues in participationist categories as well, but the forensic statements begin to gain prominence. There is more of a focus on forgiveness and imputation, without losing the language of participation. Perhaps Mannermaa does not pay enough attention to Luther's forensic language, though if this is the case he does so only because of its overemphasis in other treatments of Luther's theology.

Though it has been demonstrated that many aspects of Mannermaa's reading are correct, there are still a few problems with his thesis: First, Mannermaa's contention that ontological union is part of what Luther means when discussing the concept of justification seems to be contradicted by several statements of Luther. Though they are connected concepts, Luther often distinguishes ontological union and justification: "Therefore the Christ who

52. *LW* 26:11.

is grasped by faith and who lives in the heart is the true Christian righteousness, on account of which God counts us righteous and grants us eternal life."[53] Union with Christ is not justification, but is the basis for justification.[54] It is the ontological grounding for imputation and forgiveness. Thus the Formula of Concord is in agreement with Luther in distinguishing these as two separate blessings of grace.

Secondly, though Christ is grasped by and present in faith according to Luther, Mannermaa goes too far in saying that, for Luther, Christ is faith. Luther does not see faith as an uncreated grace, but a creation in the believer's heart by the Holy Spirit: "This is why we continually teach that the knowledge of Christ and of faith is not a human work but utterly a divine gift; as God creates faith, so He preserves us in it."[55] Several statements in the Galatians commentary make similar references to faith as created.

Third, Mannermaa misses Luther's eschatological focus. It is not simply the second person of the Trinity, or even the incarnate Christ, but the resurrected Christ who is present in faith. Through union with the resurrected Son of God, the believer participates in the kingdom of God. This is the basis for the Christian's justification, regeneration, and sanctification. They are gifts of the kingdom of God breaking into the present age through the presence of the resurrected Christ. Apart from communion with the resurrected Christ, one does not participate in the kingdom of God and thus has no salvation. This explains Luther's constant insistence on the omnipresence of Christ's human nature, especially as

53. *LW* 26:129.

54. Mannermaa's claim may be correct in reference to the young Luther. For example, in his 1519 Galatians lectures he comments: "This faith justifies you; it will cause Christ to dwell, live, and reign in you" (*LW* 27:172).

55. *LW* 26:64.

*Which Luther?*

received in the Eucharist. For Luther, a symbolic or even a Calvinistic view of the Supper separates the human Christ from his people and thus the ontological grounding for God's gracious imputation is lost. An ontological union with the resurrected Christ is necessary for justification.

Finally, Mannermaa's tendency to pit Luther's own theology of works against that of the later Lutheran confessional documents is overstated. In his article "Luther and Theosis,"[56] Kurt Marquart argues that aspects of Mannermaa's approach to justification, specifically his contention that union with Christ precedes justification, do not conflict with the Formula of Concord's denial of the Osiandrian view of justification. As Marquart writes, "Actually the opposition between 'in us' and 'outside' of us is a rule of thumb rather than a precise doctrinal definition. Its intent is certainly correct, but as a form of words it is neither taught by the Formula, nor does it belong to the *status controversiae*, the point at issue, in the Osiandrian dispute."[57] He also points out that "only the Osiandrian justification-by-indwelling-righteousness is rejected."[58] Thus the Lutheran reformers did not reject the indwelling of Christ as an aspect of justification, but only Osiander's contention of divine indwelling to the neglect of the human nature and the legal aspects of justification.[59]

## IMPLICATIONS

Beyond the ecumenical implications Mannermaa and others have pointed out, this new look at Luther challenges many

56. Marquart, "Luther and Theosis."
57. Ibid., 200.
58. Ibid.
59. I would add to this that Osiander viewed justification as a process that Luther, aside from a few ambiguous statements, does not do.

assumptions in modern Pauline scholarship. The Lutheran reading of Paul that has been critiqued is not truly Lutheran at all, but a caricature of the reformer. There are several ways in which this picture of Luther should be corrected.

First, rather than being merely the son of late medieval piety as is claimed by Stendahl, Luther is shown to be thoroughly consistent with patristic thought in his christological considerations that underlie his approach to the gospel. Luther was not the individualistic Bible interpreter he has been portrayed as in polemical contexts. The *analogia fidei* played a large role in his theological considerations, as he consistently emphasized the importance of the ecumenical creeds of the church.[60] For Luther, man is justified *sola fide* because faith alone unites him to Christ. Man does not need to participate in his own salvation because Christ, being very God of very God, has infinite righteousness and merit. He has the full ability and power to save apart from human work. Along with Athanasius, Luther can speak of salvation in participationist terms (i.e. sharing in divinity through union with Christ) as well as in forensic language (i.e. Athanasius' language of paying the "debt of death" all men owe to God because of Adam's transgression).

Second, Luther is placed more firmly in the German mystical tradition of the late Middle Ages. His theology is not the product of a reaction to late medieval nominalism.[61] If the primary image for justification in Luther's early writing is that of the bride and the soul and the sharing of attributes between Christ and the believer, Luther's views

---

60. This is seen in that Luther does not argue for the Chalcedonian definition of Christology. He rather assumes this in his defense of other doctrines. His treatises *On the Councils and the Church* and *The Three Symbols or Creeds of the Christian Faith* make the point rather well.

61. For the nominalist thesis, see Oberman, *Dawn of the Reformation*.

*Which Luther?*

appear to be in line with a large strand of medieval theology. Many of Luther's confessed influences spoke of salvation as the sharing of attributes between the bride and groom. This includes such a diverse group as Bernard of Clairvaux, John Tauler, John Gerson, and Johann Staupitz. The question that faced Luther was: if the groom shares his righteousness with the bride, and this righteousness is infinite and complete, what need is there for human merit? Luther saw an inconsistency in two strands of Catholic tradition, thus he gave up what he thought was inconsistent with St. Paul's teaching about righteousness.

Third, it demonstrates that common distinctions and assumed similarities between Luther and Calvin are incorrect. If this interpretation of Luther is correct, he and Calvin[62] are placed on two fundamentally different grounds. Luther stands in a consistent line with the early church and medieval tradition on many important soteriological points. For Luther, God's grace is mediated through the sacraments; for Calvin, the sacraments are covenantal signs and seals, but do not themselves give grace to the recipient. For Luther, there are both ontological and forensic aspects to salvation; for Calvin, salvation is primarily forensic. For Luther, justification includes both imputation and spiritual resurrection;[63] for Calvin justification is purely a forensic term. For Luther, sanctification is the outworking of justifi-

---

62. I recognize of course that Luther never met or talked with Calvin, though Melancthon's resistance to showing Calvin's letters to Luther point to the fact that he would have had the same attitude toward Calvin as he had with Zwingli. I use Calvin as my example simply because he is the most clear, and important, of any of the early Reformed theologians. I could just as easily use the same comparisons with Bucer.

63. This is done, not through conflating justification and sanctification, but through teaching the effective nature of God's justifying word. The forensic verdict is active.

cation connected so intimately that the terms are sometimes interchangeable; for Calvin, justification and sanctification are two separate benefits given through union with Christ. For Luther, the goal of the Christian life is giving up one's own will as alien righteousness grows, causing Christ to dwell more fully in the believer; for Calvin, the goal of the Christian life is greater obedience to God's law. For Luther, salvation comes through the presence of the resurrected Christ communicating himself to the believer; for Calvin, Christ's human nature is absent and salvation is primarily mediated through the Holy Spirit.[64]

Finally, N. T. Wright's criticism of Luther's doctrine of imputed righteousness is shown to be flawed in that it does not address the issue Luther is dealing with in his commentaries on the epistles of Paul. Wright famously states, "If we use the language of the law court, it makes no sense whatever to say that the judge imputes, imparts, bequeaths, conveys or otherwise transfers his righteousness to either the plaintiff or the defendant. Righteousness is not an object, a substance or a gas which can be passed across the courtroom."[65] Luther, however, does not see righteousness as something that can be passed around in a law court. This is to separate righteousness from Christ himself, something Luther never does. This idea is the creation of seventeenth-century scholasticism.

For Luther, the law court is sometimes not even the most appropriate model to use in discussing justification. Certainly some aspects of salvation are described with legal imagery. For example, in discussing the law, Luther uses the

---

64. There is further evidence of the disagreement between the two reformers in the fact that the book that Luther held most highly as a precursor to his own ideas, the *Theologia Germanica*, Calvin considered dangerous and mistaken.

65. Wright, *What Saint Paul Really Said*, 98.

image of man standing guilty under a righteous judge for breaking his commands. However, Luther can also describe sin as existence in the kingdom of the world in which one is under the power of Satan; it is participation in Adam. In the same way, Luther uses several different images to describe the gospel. He can speak of legal pardon for ones offenses. However, he also speaks of salvation as the reception of eschatological blessing and participation in Christ.

The problem with Wright's criticism is that he tries to fit Luther's concept of justification into a specifically legal framework. However, this is not something that Luther (or St. Paul for that matter) does, nor does he try to. One certainly does not have an ontological union with one's judge either, but that does not make it untrue. This is taking the metaphor too far.

## CONCLUSION

The evidence warrants the conclusion that Luther's doctrine of justification is not identical with the later scholastic doctrine that Stendahl, Dunn, and Wright portray. For Luther, justification is based on a prior union between the believer and Christ. This union includes a giving of Christ's person as the resurrected Son of God. In this union, the two parties are so closely linked as to be called one person. There is then an exchange of attributes wherein Christ takes the believer's sin on himself, and the believer receives Christ's very righteousness and thereby is forgiven, imputed as righteous, and reborn. The indwelling Christ then sustains the believer in faith, causing him to perform good works. Both his justification and sanctification are the work of alien righteousness. It is all a monergistic act of pure grace.

# 5

# The Apostolic Fathers

Now that both the New Perspective on Paul and Luther's doctrine of justification have been presented, the church fathers can be analyzed with reference to these two divergent interpretations of Paul. Do the earliest Christians adopt a view of Paul akin to that of the New Perspective on Paul, or of Luther?

For the apostolic fathers, the doctrine of justification arises within soteriological contexts, and most often with the individual in view. References to ecclesiology and covenant membership are absent when justification is discussed. If this is the case, then Luther's reading of Paul was not merely the result of late medieval debates concerning "righteousness," but rather an expression of theological conservation consistent with the second-century Pauline interpreters.

## CLEMENT OF ROME

Three apostolic fathers have been selected for the present discussion: Clement, Ignatius, and the anonymous author

*The Apostolic Fathers*

of the *Epistle to Diognetus*. Of the various early post-apostolic texts, these contain the most explicit and extensive discussions of the Pauline themes relevant to the present discussion.

The epistle of Clement to the Corinthians (AD 95–98),[1] usually identified as 1 *Clement*, holds a prominent place in discussions about early Christian soteriology. Apart from possibly the *Didache*, 1 *Clement* is the earliest non-canonical Christian writing. Contemporaneous with the apostolic era, it was often read in public worship, and was included in some collections of the New Testament.[2] Clement's influence upon succeeding centuries of interpreters shows that his understanding of Paul was formative for the early church's interpretation of the Pauline texts.

Though the exact identity and background of Clement of Rome remains unknown, his testimony carried weight for the early church because he shows great familiarity with the Pauline epistles. Assuming the Pastoral Epistles and Ephesians to be genuinely Pauline, Clement is the earliest source of the church's reflections on the Pauline literature.[3]

Though Clement's first epistle consists principally of ethical exhortation, he does briefly comment on Pauline soteriology. There are two instances in which Clement

1. A good introduction to Clement's epistle can be found in Nunn, "Background of the Epistle of Clement." A notable objection to the traditional dating can be found in John A. T. Robinson's *Redating the New Testament*, where he proposes a dating of early AD 70. Robinson's argument, while demonstrating that dating of patristic sources is often not as straight forward as is sometimes assumed, fails to be convincing.

2. It was included, though incomplete, in the fifth-century *Codex Alexandrinus*. The authority of Clement was such that other writings were given a Clementine title so as to defend the authority of these books.

3. A full treatment of Clement's use of scripture can be found in Mayer, "Clement of Rome and His Use of Scripture."

addresses the subject of justification. Significantly however, neither instance occurs within discussions of the familial status shared by Jews and Gentiles in the new covenant. In the same vein as Luther, Clement proposes that justification is a soteriological term and is received by faith, apart from meritorious works. In Clementine soteriology, the Pauline conception of "works of the law" is broadened beyond Mosaic commandments to negate all so-called good works from the individual's justification. Clement's doctrine of justification comports with Luther, not the NPP.[4]

## Clement on Justification

Commentators agree that Clement wrote to a divided church in Corinth. Though the exact issue is not disclosed in the epistle, it is apparent that the Corinthians were denigrated into fractions. In Corinth there was prolific pride, arrogance, and hostility. Thus the contents of Clements epistle are principally ethical. Clementine soteriology, therefore, must be extracted from his dual references to justification. Both occasions appear within the same section of the text between chapters 28–32. In these chapters, Clement encourages the Corinthians toward humility and obedience by citing several examples from important Old Testament figures.

Clement continually reminds his readers through several Old Testament texts that they are a holy nation. Because they are "a portion of the Holy One,"[5] Clement exhorts his readers to "do all the things that pertain to

---

4. Charles Merritt Neilson also argues for a Reformational understanding of Clement, agreeing with my assessment in many essential points, though he stresses an inconsistency that I do not find in Clement. See Neilson, "Clement of Rome and Moralism."

5. *1 Clem.* 29:1, in *Apostolic Fathers*.

*The Apostolic Fathers*

holiness, forsaking slander, disgusting and impure embraces, drunkenness and rioting and detestable lusts, abominable adultery, detestable pride."[6] The Corinthians are to "join with those to whom grace is given by God."[7] Clement's first statement on justification is situated in this context: "Let us clothe ourselves in concord, being humble and self-controlled, keeping ourselves far from all backbiting and slander, being justified by works and not by words (ἔργοις δικαιούμενοι καὶ μὴ λόγοις)."[8] This statement has been used to argue that Clement believed Christians can achieve salvation by their works in contrast to a Lutheran conception of *sola fide*. However, the context of Clement's argument demonstrates consistency with Luther, rather than an early form of merit theology.

In a Pauline fashion, Clement begins this section by recalling the Corinthians' status as those chosen by God. *Because* they are God's chosen people, Αγίου ουν μερις υπάρχοντες ποιήσωμεν τα του αγιασμου πάντα,[9] they must do that which is in accord with holiness (φεύγοντες καταλαλιάς.) [10] Clement is basing his imperative upon the indicative. Because Clement implements the term δικαιούμενο within this context after assuring his readers of their covenantal identity, justification likely has an evidential meaning. Works serve to vindicate one's covenant status; they do not determine it. This is further articulated by the fact that Clement speaks about the "testimony to our good deeds"[11] by others, thus distinguishing one's vindication

6. *1 Clem.* 30:1.

7. *1 Clem.* 30:3.

8. *1 Clem.* 30:3.

9. "Seeing then that we are a portion of one who is holy" (*1 Clem.* 30:1).

10. "Let us do all the works of sanctification" (*1 Clem.* 30:1).

11. *1 Clem.* 30:7.

before men from justification before God. Nothing soteriological appears in the immediate context.

For Clement, the term "justification" may refer, as Wright defines the term, to "one's status as a member of God's covenant people."[12] This is apparent in his use of the term within the context of vindication. Notwithstanding, it is noteworthy that discussion of Jew-Gentile familial relations is absent. Clement reminds his readers that, like the patriarchs, they must evidence behavior commensurate with their election. This use of the term is not unique with Clement or the NPP, but is in keeping with Paul's theology of Christian obedience and Luther's concept of double justification.

Clement continues his admonition by referencing specific examples throughout redemptive history. Abraham was blessed "because he attained righteousness and truth through faith";[13] Isaac "went willingly to be sacrificed";[14] and Jacob went to serve Laban "[w]ith humility."[15] After describing the abundance of God's gifts to Jacob, including the priesthood and the lineage through which Christ would come, Clement writes for the second time about justification:

> And so we, having been called through his will in Christ Jesus, are not justified through themselves or their own works or the righteous actions that they did, but through his will. And so we, having been called through his will in Christ Jesus, are not justified through ourselves or our own wisdom or understanding or piety, or works that we have done in

12. Wright, *Paul in Fresh Perspective*, 113.
13. *1 Clem.* 31:2.
14. *1 Clem.* 31:3.
15. *1 Clem.* 31:4.

holiness of heart, but through faith, by which the Almighty God has justified all who have existed from the beginning; to whom be the glory for ever and ever. Amen.[16]

The semantic contact of the terms δικαιούμεθα, ἔργων, and πίστεως establishes a connection with Pauline discussions of justification, especially as explicated in Galatians and Romans.[17] Both writers claim justification is the result of faith to the exclusion of works. Thus, this statement of Clement has implications for understanding the Pauline interpretation of Clement in reference to the NPP.

Clement does not describe justification in an explicitly covenantal context, as does the NPP, but with the goal to encourage humility. Discussions of Christian identity and Jewish law keeping are completely absent. Thus, as in Luther, the Clementine doctrine of justification transcends the subject of ecclesiology and covenant membership. Clement expounds justification not within a discussion of table fellowship, but within a discourse about "the magnificence of the gifts that are given by God."[18] This demonstrates that Clement uses the doctrine of justification by faith to prompt humility in his readers. He does so by explaining that justification is God's great gift, received not "through ourselves" but "through his will in Christ Jesus."[19] As Luther would later recognize,[20] there is a contrast between man's act and God's act in justification.

16. *1 Clem.* 32:3–4.

17. Clement's view of faith is also greatly influenced by the book of Hebrews, and likely James. See Bacon, "Doctrine of Faith in Hebrews."

18. *1 Clem.* 32:1.

19. *1 Clem.* 32:3.

20. *LW* 26:8: "In other words, this is the righteousness of Christ and of the Holy Spirit, which we do not perform but receive which we

## The Righteousness of One

Consistent with a Lutheran reading of Paul, justification for Clement occurs through faith apart from good works. Clement does not limit the Pauline polemic against works to Jewish ceremonial works, as is the tendency in the NPP. They are not confined to "Sabbath, food-laws, circumcision,"[21] or other Mosaic commands. For Clement, works include: "wisdom" (σοφίας), "piety" (εὐσεβείας), and "works that we have done out of holiness of heart" (ἔργων ὧν κατειργασάμεθα ἐν ὁσιότητι καρδίας). These good deeds are contrasted with πίστεως, creating a works/faith distinction in Clementine soteriology; faith justifies apart from all pious deeds. For Clement, justification is based upon faith only. Clement thus holds to *sola fide* in a Reformation sense.

This is further evidenced by the charge of antinomianism anticipated by Clement. Immediately following his statement on justification by faith, Clement writes:

> What shall we do, brothers? Shall we idly abstain from doing good, and forsake love? May the Master never allow this to happen, at least to us; but let us hasten with earnestness and zeal to accomplish every good work. For the Creator and Master of the universe himself rejoices in his works.[22]

As is common when the gospel of free grace is proclaimed, Clement expects that some would use the doctrine of justification by faith as a license to sin. If Clement propounded justification in a non-soteriological context, this defense would be unnecessary. Such questions would not arise in the framework of familial identity. Had Clement not intended to exclude *all* works from one's justification,

---

do not have but accept, when God the Father grants it to us through Jesus Christ."

21. Wright, *What Saint Paul Really Said*, 132.

22. *1 Clem.* 33:1–2.

*The Apostolic Fathers*

his response would differ. This would occasion a mention of works that do justify, had this been Clement's belief. However, in a "Lutheran" fashion, Clement answers simply: "For the Creator and Master of the universe himself rejoices in his works."[23]

## Torrance: Justification through Self-Abasement

T. F. Torrance claims that, for Clement, justification by faith is understood as "self-abasement as a righteous act."[24] Justification by faith does not mean that faith saves because it grasps Christ (*pace* Luther); rather, Clement understands faith as man's act of self-abasement and humility, which justifies due to its inherent goodness. Thus, according to Torrance's reading of Clement, man is justified by his own actions. This would negate a correspondence between Clement and Luther on the doctrine of justification. There are several reasons to doubt Torrance's reading of Clement.

First, it is anachronistic to ask Clement to think about late medieval views on justification that understood self-abasement as a righteous act. For Luther, late medieval theology had replaced Jewish works (circumcision, Sabbath keeping, etc.) with other righteous works as meritorious—and therefore justifying. These works included self-impoverishment, self-affliction, material deprivation, and various other works of apparent humility. Clement likely would not assume that acts of humility could somehow be meritorious. Torrance[25] expects Clement to be more specified in his

23. *1 Clem.* 33:2.

24. Torrance, *Doctrine of Grace in the Apostolic Fathers*, 50.

25. This type of anachronism is common in Torrance's work. For example Torrance disavows all statements of conditionality as a distortion of Paulinism. This is not due to his adherence to a Reformational understanding of Paul, but of Barthian objectivism.

language than was necessary for a first century Christian. This is an example of not allowing Clement to speak for himself, and forcing medieval categories into his thought.

Second, the context negates this interpretation. Before making his second statement about justification, Clement presents examples of the patriarchs' humility. He demonstrates the virtues of the fathers of Israel through specific acts. Notice, however, the example listed by Clement immediately preceding his statement on justification, namely Jacob. Clement does not mention any virtuous action of Jacob. Significantly, he points to God's promise: "For from Jacob came all the priests and Levites who minister at the altar of God; from him comes the Lord Jesus according to the flesh."[26] There is no reference to Jacob's self-abasement in the immediate context. Clement proposes that as the great heroes of the Old Covenant were humble, so to should Christians be humble because they likewise are justified apart from meritorious works. It is not that humility yields justification. The context of Clement's second justification statement (32:3–4) demonstrates that justification is not achieved by self-abasement, but by faith alone.

Finally, the Clementine statement on justification conclusively shows that justification cannot be achieved by works of humility. Clement states that Christians are not "justified through themselves or their own works or the righteous actions that they did, but through his will. And so we, having been called through his will in Christ Jesus, are not justified through ourselves or our own wisdom or understanding or piety, or works that we have done in holiness of heart."[27] Clement excludes works in the discussion of justification. There are insufficient grounds to conclude that the "works that we have done in holiness of heart"

26. *1 Clem.* 32:2.
27. *1 Clem.* 32:3–4.

would preclude acts of self-abasement. In fact, Clement's entire epistle is written to urge the Corinthians toward good works of humility. It is incommensurate with the tenor of this epistle that acts of self-abasement would not be categorized under "works that we have done in holiness of heart," which, according to Clement, do not justify. Good works as such do not justify, including works of humility.

## Conclusion

Though Clement uses the term "justification" as a term of identification as does Wright (though still without explicit covenantal terminology), he also employs the term in a manner analogous to Luther. Both Clement and Luther regard justification as a soteriological term that is not limited in its scope to Jew-Gentile discussions. In contrast to Wright, for Clement and Luther, justification does not refer primarily to ecclesiology.[28] For both Clement and Luther, the Pauline polemic against works does not refer only to Jewish boundary markers, but to good works in general. If Clement were asked what works a man must perform to achieve justification, he would likely respond as did Luther: "Nothing at all."[29]

### IGNATIUS OF ANTIOCH

Ignatius was the bishop of Antioch in the beginning of the second century. He apparently was a figure of some repute

---

28. Wright, *What Saint Paul Really Said*, 119: "In standard Christian theological language, [Justification] wasn't so much about soteriology as about ecclesiology; not so much about salvation as about the church."

29. *LW* 26:4.

## The Righteousness of One

in the early church, a friend of Polycarp and possible acquaintance of Peter and John. He was martyred, according to the testimony of Eusebius, under the reign of Trajan (AD 98–117). The precise date is likely to remain a mystery. On his way to Rome to be martyred, Ignatius wrote six letters to churches and one to his friend Polycarp.[30] Throughout the Middle Ages, several spurious works appeared being attached to the prominent figure's name, along with three different recensions of his genuine epistles and a few mythological accounts of his martyrdom.[31] That there were various spurious works were attached to his name testifies to the prominence of this figure in both the early and medieval church. Thus his theology was highly influential in formulating the teaching of the early church, and consequently, his reading of Paul.

Ignatius has often been studied in conjunction with the early organization of the Christian church, and especially the rise of the monarchical bishop. His significance also lies in his high Christology, which at times sounds almost post-Nicene.[32] Though these concepts may be most central in Ignatius' mind, due to his role in the church's earliest christological controversies, soteriological discussion is far from absent.

Though Torrance claims that Ignatian theology is "Corrupted partly by the ordinary Hellenistic connotation and partly by Gnostic-Judaistic thought, as well as

---

30. Though occasionally the authenticity of all or some of these letters have been questioned. See, for example, Schoedel, "Are the Letters of Ignatius of Antioch Authentic?" The argument for inauthenticity, however, has not gained wide acceptance.

31. For more on the background of Ignatius, see Barnard, "Background of St. Ignatius of Antioch."

32. This of course arises in his debates with early Gnosticism. An evaluation of the heresies dealt with by Ignatius can be found in Molland, "Heretics Combatted by Ignatius of Antioch."

by a failure to apprehend the fundamental significance of the death of Christ,"[33] a more cautious reading yields the conclusion that Ignatian soteriology is thoroughly consistent with Luther's reading of the Pauline epistles. Ignatius approaches Luther's understanding of Paul in attaching fundamental significance to faith, as well as placing justification within the context of individual salvation. Though Ignatius often references the relationship between Christianity and Judaism, these discussions lack any mention of justification in the manner proposed by NPP proponents. Ignatius also approaches Luther's soteriology in attaching primary significance to the sacramental life, and ontological union with Christ.

## Ignatius on Justification

Like Clement, Ignatius' epistles contain only two brief statements that use the term "justification." Neither is extensive and neither explicitly defines the term. The first occurs in his epistle to the Romans:

> From Syria all the way to Rome I am fighting with wild beasts, on land and sea, by night and day, chained amidst ten leopards (that is a company of soldiers) who only get worse when they all are well treated. Yet because of their mistreatment I am becoming more of a disciple; nevertheless I am not thereby justified.[34]

In the above quote, Ignatius is using the term "justified" (δεδικαίωμαι) to mean something approximating "vindicated" or "acquitted."[35] Final judgment is likely in view as

33. Torrance, *Doctrine of Grace*, 89.

34. Rom 5:1.

35. This is similar to the way Paul uses the term in 1 Cor 4:4:

he is referencing a common Ignatian theme: initiation as a disciple begins when one suffers for the sake of the gospel, and this discipleship is consummated through martyrdom. His mistreatment by soldiers has begun the path of righteous suffering which will climax with justification at death. A discussion of Jew-Gentile table fellowship is significantly absent. This is a noteworthy omission, had Ignatius read Paul in the same vein as the NPP.

The eschatological backdrop of justification can be seen more clearly in Ignatius' second statement on the subject:

> Moreover, I urge you to do nothing in a spirit of contentiousness, but in accordance with the teaching of Christ. For I heard some people say, "If I do not find it in the archives, I do not believe it in the gospel." And when I said to them, "It is written," they answered me, "That is precisely the question." But for me, the "archives" are Jesus Christ, the unalterable archives are his cross and death and his resurrection and the faith that comes through him; by these things I want, through your prayers, to be justified.[36]

In this instance, Ignatius' statement on justification does come within the context of Jewish and Christian relations.[37] However, he is not answering the question of ethnicity and covenant identification. The issue he is discussing is that of the Old Testament scriptures. For the objector, the

---

"For I am not aware of anything against myself, but I am not thereby acquitted. It is the Lord who judges me."

36. Ignatius, *Phld.* 8:2.

37. Several articles have been written on Ignatius' view of Judaism. One I have found particularly insightful is Barrett, "Jews and Judaizers in the Epistles of Ignatius."

*The Apostolic Fathers*

Old Testament is the highest source of revelation; for Ignatius revelation is to be found primarily in Christ.

Justification itself is propounded by Ignatius as a future event: "In this, I desire through your prayers, to be justified (ἐν οἷσ θέλω ἐν τῇ προσευχῇ ὑμῶν δικαιωθῆναι)."[38] It is achieved through the death and resurrection of Christ (σταυρόσ αὐτοῦ καί ὁ θάνατοσ καί ἡ ἀνάστασιζ),[39] faith (πίστις), and the prayers of his readers (προσευχῇ ὑμῶν).[40] The concepts of prayer and eschatology, as used here, are prominent themes in Ignatian soteriology. He can state in a similar way: "Remember me in your prayers, in order that I may reach God."[41] Once again, in a parallel passage Ignatius writes: "Let nothing appeal to you apart from him, in whom I carry around these chains (my spiritual pearls!), by which I hope, through your prayers, to rise again."[42] Ignatius' petitions for prayer are always in view of his resurrection; thus, as his statement on justification directly parallels these discussions of resurrection, justification and resurrection are likely synonymous terms. For Ignatius, justification *is* resurrection—or is at least a related eschatological concept.

Though this may vindicate Wright's claim that "Justification for Paul cannot be understood apart from eschatology,"[43] Ignatius contradicts Wright's view that redemption is primarily about the cosmos as a whole. Ignatius centers on the resurrection of individuals; he consistently references his own resurrection and that of his readers without reference to the redemption of the cosmos.[44]

38. Ignatius, *Phld.* 8:2.
39. Ibid.
40. Ibid.
41. Ignatius, *Magn.* 14:1.
42. Ignatius, *Eph.* 11:2.
43. Wright, *What Saint Paul Really Said*, 117.
44. This is not to suggest that Ignatius did not view redemption

# The Righteousness of One

## Justification by Faith

Though there is no indication that Ignatius would either affirm or deny Luther's understanding of justification by faith *alone*, Ignatius does gives primacy to faith as the central subjective element of salvation. Ignatius is content to describe justification resulting from faith without mention of works; Ignatius hopes in "his cross and death and his resurrection and the faith that comes through him; by these things I want, through your prayers, to be justified."[45] Ignatius consistently gives primacy to faith, and most often with the salvation of his readers in view. Faith is not a badge of covenant membership, but a means of receiving soteric benefits. Jesus died "for us in order that by believing in his death you might escape death."[46] He writes again to the Trallians that God will "raise up in Christ Jesus us who believe in him."[47] Writing about the salvation of the Old Testament saints he can say that "Because they also believed in him, they were saved."[48] Faith is at least the *central* personal aspect of salvation for Ignatius, and is not primarily a badge of covenant membership.

Ignatius consistently emphasizes the cohesion of faith and resurrection. Believing unites one to Christ, especially his resurrection, and secures the Christian's resurrection. Jesus "was raised from the dead when his Father raised him up. In the same way his Father will likewise also raise up in Christ Jesus us who believe in him. Apart from him we

---

as a cosmic event, but to show that the salvation of individual Christians takes precedence over God's act of renewal within creation as a whole.

45. Ignatius, *Phld.* 8:2.
46. Ignatius, *Trall.* 2:1.
47. Ibid., 9:2.
48. Ignatius, *Phld.* 5:2.

*The Apostolic Fathers*

have no true life."[49] Since Ignatius equates justification and resurrection, it is not unwarranted to claim a doctrine of justification by faith in Ignatius. Luther expounds the doctrine of justification in similar terms: "Therefore, the resurrection of Christ is our righteousness and our life, not only by way of an example but also by virtue of its power. Apart from Christ's resurrection no one can rise, no matter how many good works he does."[50] Luther tends to emphasize the past and present aspects of justification, whereas Ignatian theology stresses its eschatological nature.

Ignatius does not shift all of Christian salvation into the future age. He does infrequently testify to a more "Lutheran" perspective by considering eternal life a present reality inaugurated by the advent of Christ: "God appeared in human form to bring the newness of eternal life; As a result, all things were thrown into ferment, because the abolition of death was being carried out."[51] For Ignatius, salvation is consummated only at the resurrection, though one begins to obtain its benefits in the present age through union with the resurrected Christ. Luther can purport similarly that, "Our being justified perfectly still remains to be seen, and this is what we hope for. Thus our righteousness does not yet exist in fact, but it still exists in hope."[52] Both Luther and Ignatius would agree with Wright that "It is 'justification' in the present, anticipating the verdict of the future. God will declare on the last day that certain people are "in the right," by raising them from the dead; and that verdict has been brought forward into the present."[53] However, in contrast to Wright, the focus for Luther and Ignatius is on

49. Ignatius, *Trall.* 9:2.
50. *LW* 27.
51. Eph 19:3.
52. *LW* 27:21.
53. Wright, *Justification*, 147.

the individual's reception of this salvation, rather than the cosmos as a whole.

## Union with Christ

Corresponding to Luther's consistent emphasis on union with Christ, Ignatius' theology is fundamentally mystical. Whether he is discussing ecclesiology, Christology, or holy living, Ignatius cannot fail to mention the union that the Christian has with Christ. He anticipates Luther's 1535 Galatians commentary in expounding upon union as the ontological grounding for subsequent benefits of salvation.

For Ignatius, the Christian life is grounded in union with God. Christians are "God-bearers and temple-bearers, Christ-bearers, bearers of holy things, adorned in every respect with the commandments of Jesus Christ."[54] For one to receive grace, he must "be found in Christ Jesus."[55] Doing so is participation in eternal life. Only in Christ, as one participates in God, will one be found guiltless upon his advent. He is "our true life."[56] For Ignatius, the ethical life is also only achievable through union: "Let no one regard his neighbor in merely human terms, but in Jesus Christ love one another always."[57] Luther echoes this Ignatian theme stating that "Christ and my conscience must become one body, so that nothing remains in my sight but Christ, crucified and risen."[58] Participation in Christ is the central soteriological motif for Ignatius and is the foundation of the Christian life, as it is for Luther.

---

54. Ignatius, *Eph.* 9:2.
55. Ibid., 11:1.
56. Ignatius, *Smyrn.* 4:2.
57. Ignatius, *Magn.* 6:2.
58. *LW* 26:167.

Direct communion with God is not an individualistic enterprise for Ignatius. It occurs primarily within the context of public worship, especially as one is in communion with the local bishop.

> You must join this chorus, every one of you, so that by being harmonious in unanimity and taking your pitch from God you may sing in unison with one voice through Jesus Christ to the Father, in order that he may both hear you and, on the basis of what you do well, acknowledge that you are members of his Son. It is, therefore, advantageous for you to be in perfect unity, on order that you may always have a share in God.[59]

The unity of the church in corporate worship is a picture of the unity of the Father and Son, as well as of Christ and his bride. Significantly, Ignatius' concept of corporate worship transcends the concept of a symbolic representation. The unity of Christ and the church occurs in the context of, and through, worship. Participation in the fellowship and eternal unity of Father and Son also occurs within the milieu of corporate worship.

It is significant that justification is not mentioned in these frequent Ignatian ecclesial discussions. This would be a glaring omission if Ignatius' comprehended the Pauline concept in a manner commensurate with Wright, who states that the Pauline use of justification "always had in mind God's declaration of membership."[60] If this were Ignatius' understanding, the topic of justification would arise in his several ecclesial discussions.

---

59. Ignatius, Eph. 4:2.
60. Wright, *Justification*, 116.

# The Righteousness of One

## Good Works

Contrary to the present argument, T. F. Torrance argues that Ignatius, in contrast to Luther, misunderstands the Pauline doctrine of justification by faith, and believes that "Justification is a matter of faith and love, or of faith and works."[61] Though a cursory reading may yield this conclusion, a careful examination reveals a more complex pattern of thought consistent with Luther.

Ignatius never attributes justification to works. Faith is always associated with justification, which, as argued previously, is identical with resurrection. Ignatius never pronounces that the Christian is justified, or will be resurrected, by good works or an act of love.

In the theology of Ignatius, good works are seen as the consequence of God's gift of salvation for the individual, not the basis:

> Those who belong to the flesh cannot do spiritual things, nor can those who are spiritual do fleshly things, just as faith cannot do the things of unfaithfulness, nor unfaithfulness the things of faith. Moreover, even those things that you do according to the flesh are in fact spiritual, for you do everything in Jesus Christ.[62]

Once more, union takes precedence in Ignatius' thought. Faith unites one to Christ. Reception of the status of being "in Jesus Christ" generates a renewed nature. The new man no longer lives according to sinful desires, but in accordance with the Spirit. Corresponding to Luther's imagery,[63] Ignatius employs the analogy of a tree and its fruit:

61. Torrance, *Doctrine of Grace*, 68.
62. Ignatius, Eph. 8:2.
63. LW 26:255: "Thus he is a true doer of the Law who receives

No one professing faith sins, nor does anyone possessing love hate. The tree is known by its fruit; thus those who profess to be Christ's will be recognized by their actions. For the work is a matter not of what one promises now, but of persevering to the end in the power of faith.[64]

For Ignatius, good works are the product of being identified with Christ, not the source, and are always performed in the power of faith.

Finally, though Ignatius emphasizes love in some soteric contexts, he does not understand love as a meritorious act. Torrance uses the following quote to justify his conclusion: "[Y]ou are the stones of a temple, prepared beforehand by the building of God the Father, hoisted up to the heights by the crane of Jesus Christ, which is the cross, using as a rope the Holy Spirit; your faith is what lifts you up, and love is the way that leads up to God."[65] Ignatius does emphasize the unity of faith and love in several other statements as well. However, Ignatius does not identify love as a meritorious act; love is not even an act at all. It is a bond of affection that initiates dwelling with God in the unity of Father and Son.[66] Love is never connected with actions in the Ignatian epistles, but appears in conjunction with faith as an almost synonymous term and is always directed toward Christ.[67]

---

the Holy Spirit through faith in Christ and then begins to love God and to do good to his neighbor. Hence "to do" includes faith at the same time. Faith takes the doer himself and makes him into a tree, and his deeds become fruit. First there must be a tree, then the fruit."

64. Ignatius, *Eph.* 14:2.

65. Ibid., 9:1.

66. "Be eager, therefore, to be firmly grounded in the precepts of the Lord and the apostles, in order that in whatever you do, you may prosper, physically and spiritually, in faith and love, in the Son and the Father and in the Spirit" (Ignatius, *Magn.* 13:1).

67. Ignatius, *Eph.* 1:1; 14:1, 20:1; *Magn.* 13:1; *Trall.* 8:1; *Phld.* 9:2;

Ignatius even appears to equate love with Christ himself.[68] Despite corresponding language, Ignatius' theology of faith and love is not identical with the prominent medieval concept of "formed faith" attacked by Luther. Ignatian theology can be harmonized with Luther's understanding of justification *sola fide*.

## Sacraments

Martin Luther's doctrine of justification was formed in connection with the sacramental life of the church. Correspondingly, Ignatius—having penned one of the earliest testimonies to the second-century church's beliefs about the sacraments—contends for a sacramental soteriology.

Ignatius assumes a realistic presence of the person of Jesus Christ in the eucharistic meal. Discussing docetic Christology, Ignatius writes that the Docetists "abstain from Eucharist and prayer because they refuse to acknowledge that the Eucharist is the flesh of our savior Jesus Christ, which suffered for our sins and which the Father by his goodness raised up."[69] Ignatius could not be more lucid in proclaiming that Christ's flesh is eaten during the eucharistic celebration. This doctrine is also positioned in the context of union with Christ, as the eating of the loaf and drinking of wine is once again a depiction of, and means of bringing about, the unity of Christ with his church:

> Take care, therefore, to participate in one Eucharist (for there is one flesh of our Lord Jesus

---

Smyrn. 6:1; 13:2.

68. "You, therefore, must arm yourselves with gentleness and regain your strength in faith (which is the flesh of the Lord) and in love (which is the blood of Jesus Christ)" (Ignatius, *Trall.* 8:1).

69. Ignatius, *Smyrn.* 6:2.

*The Apostolic Fathers*

> Christ, and one cup that leads to unity through his blood; there is one altar, just as there is one bishop, together with the council of presbyters and the deacons, my fellow servants), in order that whatever you do, you do in accordance with God.[70]

In Ignatian theology, the eucharistic meal is an important component of one's union with Christ wherein one partakes of the resurrected Christ's real body and blood, and is united with fellow believers as a cohesive humanity under Christ's lordship. It is instrumental in bringing about one's eschatological vindication—justification.[71]

Ignatius does not offer an extensive treatment of baptism in any of his seven epistles, but gives a small number of references to the practice. The clearest is not directly on baptisms in the church but Christ's. Jesus was "was born and was baptized in order that by his suffering he might cleanse the water."[72] The implication is that something significant happened to baptismal water after Christ's own baptism so that it might cleanse those who are baptized in the church.[73] Baptism is not, for Ignatius as for Luther, mere symbolism, but a means of salvation.

---

70. Ignatius, *Phld.* 4:1.

71. This is why Ignatius calls the Eucharist the "medicine of immortality" (Ignatius, Eph. 20:2).

72. Ibid., 18:2.

73. If Ignatian baptismal theology is grounded in union with Christ as is his Eucharistic theology, he would certainly agree with Luther that "Therefore Paul teaches that Baptism is not a sign but the garment of Christ, in fact, that Christ Himself is our garment. Hence Baptism is a very powerful and effective thing. For when we have put on Christ, the garment of our righteousness and salvation, then we also put on Christ, the garment of imitation" (*LW* 26).

The Righteousness of One

## Conclusion

Ignatius' doctrine of justification corresponds with Luther's in several ways. Both theologians connect justification with resurrection; with Ignatius the focus is on future resurrection, whereas for Luther emphasis lies on the spiritual resurrection in the present age. Neither theologian places justification, or faith in an ecclesiological context as does the NPP. Justification references individual salvation primarily; faith is a means of receiving soteriological benefits, not a badge of covenant membership. For both Luther and Ignatius, faith is the primary means for obtaining justification. Ignatius speaks of love as salvific, though Ignatius does not define love as a work, but a bond of affection with Christ. Ignatius and Luther describe good works as the result of salvation, not as its cause. Both theologians emphasize union with Christ as a fundamental aspect of the Christian life and the basis for all the blessings of God. Finally, Ignatius' soteriology is thoroughly sacramental, as is Luther's. While there is not an exact correspondence of Lutheran and Ignatian soteriological conceptualities, there are numerous overlapping themes.

## THE EPISTLE TO DIOGNETUS

The *Epistle to Diognetus* survives as a mysterious early work of Christian apologetics. Its author and date are unknown, though several conjectures have been made. Ancient writers attributed the work to Justin Martyr, but theological and stylistic differences make this connection improbable. Other suggested authors are Polycarp, Quadratus, and Hippolytus. None of these suggestions have gained wide acceptance, and the authorship is likely to remain a mystery.

*The Apostolic Fathers*

The dating and circumstance of the letter are equally troubling. There are no references to specific historical circumstances that give even an approximate date. However, due to the issues addressed by the author, which are those repeatedly discussed throughout the second century, it is fairly certain that the dating of the epistle ranges somewhere from the early to late second century. A more precise dating is currently impossible.

The anonymous author of *Diognetus* defends Christian claims against two prevalent belief systems in ancient Rome: Judaism and Paganism. His apologetic argumentation begins with an attack against the popular Roman religions of his era and he derides paganism for its adoration of idols made of bronze and wood. His second argument involves a disparagement of Jewish customs such as food laws, keeping the Sabbath, and circumcision for their typological nature. Following these arguments, the author begins an extended positive apologetic for the superiority of the Christian faith to contrary views.

Within this context, a statement appears that seems at first glance to have come from one of the sixteenth-century reformers. Throughout his argument, he maintains an understanding of justification consistent with Luther and directly contradicting several claims of the NPP, specifically in identifying the righteousness of God with the righteousness of Christ rather than God's covenant faithfulness.

## The Sweet Exchange

The author, in this section of his epistle (9:1–6), is answering a common objection to the Christian faith based upon its novelty. If Jesus was the promised Messiah, and the true redeemer of mankind, why did he arrive so late in history? He responds in the following manner:

## The Righteousness of One

> So then, having already planned everything in his mind together with his child, he permitted us, during the former time, to be carried away by undisciplined impulses as we desired, led astray by pleasures and lusts, not at all because he took delight in our sins, but because he was patient; not because he approved of that former season of unrighteousness, but because he was creating the present season of righteousness, in order that we who in the former time were convicted by our own deeds as unworthy of life might now by the goodness of God be made worthy, and, having clearly demonstrated our inability to enter the kingdom of God on our own, might be enabled to do so by God's power. But when our unrighteousness was fulfilled, and it had been made perfectly clear that its wages—punishment and death—were to be expected, then the season arrived during which God had decided to reveal at last his goodness and power (oh the surpassing kindness and love of God!). He did not hate us, or reject us, or bear a grudge against us; instead he was patient and forebearing; in his mercy he took upon himself our sins; he himself gave up his own Son as a ransom for us, the holy one for the lawless, the guiltless for the guilty, the just for the unjust, the incorruptible for the corruptible, the immortal for the mortal. For what else but his righteousness could cover our sins? In whom was it possible for us, the lawless and ungodly, to be justified except in the Son of God alone? O the sweet exchange, O the incomprehensible work of God, O the unexpected blessings, that the sinfulness of many should be hidden in one righteous person, while the righteousness of one should justify many sinners![74]

---

74. *Diogn.* 9:1–5.

*The Apostolic Fathers*

Several Pauline themes are expounded in this section of the epistle. The author begins his response by discussing the inability of meritorious actions to gain entrance to the kingdom of God. All men "were convicted by [their] own deeds as unworthy of life."[75] The author of *Diognetus* reveals the extent of sin without reference to the Mosaic law, placing Pauline hamartiology within a broader context than that of the Mosaic narrative. This is a significant challenge to the claim of NPP proponents that justification is primarily an answer to a specific question regarding Christian relations to Judaism and the Mosaic law.

In the second half of his response, the author of *Diognetus* offers a solution to man's universal plight. What he outlines appears to be a view of penal substitution. God himself "gave up his own Son as a ransom for us, the holy one for the lawless, the guiltless for the guilty, the just for the unjust, the incorruptible for the corruptible, the immortal for the mortal."[76] The logic of his argumentation involves a move from the death due to mankind to the death of Christ on man's behalf.[77] This argument occurs through a series of contrasts between Christ and mankind. Christ is "holy" (αγιον), "innocent" (εκακον), "righteous" (δίκαιον), "immortal" (αθάνατον), and "incorruptible" (αφθαρτον). Humankind is "lawless" (ονόμων), "guilty" (κακων), "un- righteous" (αδίκων), "mortal" (θνητον), and "corruptible" (φθαρτον). Jesus takes upon himself the penalty man incurred through these negative attributes.

75. Ibid., 9:1.

76. Ibid., 9:2.

77. The author of Diognetus would appear to accept the view Wright argues against by saying: "And that, in turn, is why the Messiah's death under the curse of the law (Galatians 3:13) is much, much more than a simplistic exchange ('We were under the curse; he took it; we go free')" (Wright, *Justification*, 1569).

## The Righteousness of One

The sins of man were "hidden in one righteous person."[78] That which belonged to man was transferred to Christ. This corresponds with Luther's belief that Christ "undertook to bear the person of all sinners and therefore was made guilty of the sins of the entire world."[79] The author of *Diognetus* teaches a doctrine of vicarious atonement.

The final section of the answer given by the author is most significant for the present discussion.

> For what else but his righteousness could have covered our sins? In whom was it possible for us, the lawless and ungodly, to be justified, except in the Son of God alone? O the sweet exchange, O the incomprehensible work of God, O the unexpected blessings, that the sinfulness of many should be hidden in the one righteous person, while the righteousness of one should justify many sinners![80]

This language corresponds with Luther's description of the great exchange wherein Christ takes man's righteousness upon himself and attributes his own righteousness to the believer. The author of *Diognetus* identifies saving righteousness with the righteousness of Christ, not God's covenant faithfulness. This directly confronts Wrights claim that "God's righteousness remains, so to speak, God's own property. It is the reason for his acting to vindicate his people. It is not the status he bestows upon them in so doing."[81] This righteousness, according to the author of *Diognetus*, is transferred from God as the acting subject to man as the recipient. It is put over sin as a covering—not infused causing inward change—and consequently results

78. *Diogn.* 9:5.
79. *LW* 26:279–80.
80. *Diogn.* 9:4–5.
81. *LW*, 31.

*The Apostolic Fathers*

in the non-imputation of sin to the believer. It would be consistent with the author's language to describe this as "alien" righteousness.

The author of *Diognetus* parallels the reception of sins by Christ, and righteousness by the Christian. The author connects the righteousness of Christ specifically with the act of justification. Justification likely means, for the author, to count one as righteous and forgiven. This is shown by his previous language of righteousness as a "covering" (καλύψαι), something external is placed over one's sin. This understanding of justification is propounded with the parallel made by the author. The sinfulness of man is imputed to Christ. He "took upon himself our sins."[82] Consistency mandates that his righteousness is imputed in the same manner. The author of *Diognetus* would agree with Luther that "It is necessary for us to have the imputation of righteousness, which comes to us on account of Christ, who is given to us and grasped by our faith." The author of *Diognetus* teaches a double imputation.

One must be cautious, however, not to read *Diognetus* anachronistically. Mention of Christ's active obedience to the law is significantly absent. No distinction is made between an active and passive aspect of the obedience of Christ. The exact identity of the righteousness of Christ is not disclosed by the author. There are two possibilities that remain probable contextually. Christ's righteousness may refer to Christ as the sinless substitute. Language of substitution and atonement are most prominent in this section of his epistle. Another likely possibility is that Christ's righteousness refers to all of the qualities that he attributes to Christ including holiness, guiltlessness, immortality, and incorruptibility. The possibility that active obedience is

---

82. *Diogn.* 9:2.

meant by the righteousness of Christ remains though there is no contextual reason to assume this identification.

## Conclusion

The amount of written material from the anonymous author of the *Epistle to Diognetus* is sparse, yet contains a more explicit and extensive discussion of the Pauline doctrine of justification than any other apostolic father, and many writers throughout the second and third centuries. There is a correspondence with Luther's understanding of Paul on many levels. First, both writers understand human sinfulness as a universal plight from which mankind must be rescued. Death is a penalty incurred through sin. Second, the theme of vicarious substitution is present in both Luther and the anonymous author of *Diognetus*. Thirdly, both theologians place the doctrine of justification within a soteriological context. Neither limits the doctrine to a covenantal or ecclesiological framework, as is its primary use in the NPP. Finally, in contrast to Wright, the author of *Diognetus* identifies God's saving righteousness with the righteousness of Christ imputed to the Christian. A more patent declaration of imputed righteousness could not have been written from the pen of Martin Luther himself.

### FINAL ASSESSMENT

The common claim of proponents of the NPP that Martin Luther's interpretation of Paul was driven by late medieval debates about righteousness has thus been exposed as having some serious deficiencies. Luther's understanding of salvation, especially through his reading of the Pauline epistles, is in many respects consistent with some of the church's earliest interpreters of Paul. Within one hundred years of the writing of Romans and Galatians, the themes that informed Luther's thought were accepted by many in the church.

In all three of the above writers, justification is placed within a soteriological context, though it may be used as a term of identification as well. For Clement, justification refers to a present reality of salvation. It is an act of God achieved by faith alone, apart from good works as a whole, not simply the Mosaic commandments. For Ignatius, justification primarily references God's act of salvation at the advent of Christ, though aspects of this can be experienced in the present age. It is achieved by faith through union with Christ; it is not accomplished by man's works. For the author of *Diognetus*, justification is an act whereby the Christian is forgiven and imputed righteous by the righteousness of Christ.

Perhaps, rather than being driven by the theological controversies of his day and his introspective conscience, Luther was brought to his theological convictions by a careful study of Paul. Of course Luther, like anyone else, was affected by his own historical setting. He may have indeed looked for answers because he had a tormented conscience and had fallen into certain medieval debates. However, it is reductionistic to assume that these factors alone drove Luther to his theological convictions. 1400 years before Luther, several of the church's most influential theologians understood Paul in a similar vein, and they could do so without a medieval context. Perhaps Luther's reading of Paul needs to be given a more honest and serious examination once again.

# 6

# Justin Martyr

It is imperative to move beyond the apostolic fathers to study other early patristic writings to understand the true weight of this issue, as it has been duly shown that the apostolic fathers agree with Luther's understanding of Paulinism, and disagree with Wright's interpretation. The earliest and most extensive Christian writings after the era of the apostolic fathers are those of Justin Martyr. Justin represents the beginning of the apologetic era in second-century Christian theology.[1] He, along with Irenaeus, provides us with the most thorough treatment of Christian teaching and practice in the era following the apostolic fathers.

Though certainly influenced by his earlier training in Greek philosophy, especially middle Platonism, Justin is a thoroughly Christian writer. His knowledge of Scripture extends to the majority of the Old Testament, and among the New Testament writings: the four Gospels, the epistles

---

1. The best lengthy treatment of Justin's theology in English is Barnard, *Justin Martyr*.

*Justin Martyr*

of Paul, Revelation, and possibly Acts, James, 1 Peter, and 1 John.[2]

While Justin is certainly no proto-Lutheran, he consistently references and comments on the Pauline epistles, giving an indication that on several levels his understanding of Paul's writings are consistent with Luther's reading over against the proposed New Perspective on Paul. While Paul's writings to the Romans and Galatians are used in connection with the relation between Jews and Gentiles in Justin, the issue of table fellowship is not understood as the core of Paul's polemic. For Justin, the salvation of individuals is at the forefront. While Justin does propose a universal restoration of creation as well, this is always a subservient goal of redemption.

It has often been stated that Justin's concept of salvation is thoroughly moralistic. On this ground, a "Lutheran" reading of Paul is negated. However, I propose that Justin's moralism has often been overstated. While Justin would not likely ascent to Luther's concept of *sola fide*, his writings do show a more christological conception of salvation than is often realized. Salvation is achieved through the death and resurrection of Christ; this is also accompanied by a union of God and man in the person of Christ, which subsequently causes the believer to participate in divinity through faith. Luther's *communicatio idiomatum* between Christ and the believer is anticipated in Justin's reading of Paul.

Justin also approaches Luther's understanding of the law over against the NPP. For Justin, the law requires perfect obedience. This obedience has been achieved by none, resulting in a universal curse over mankind. This curse brings death. Christ must take away this curse (Justin never

2. For more on Justin's canon see Skarsaune, "Justin and His Bible."

equates this curse with the exile). Salvation, therefore, for both Justin and Luther, must be achieved apart from works of the law through the work of Christ.

## JUSTIN'S CONCERN FOR INDIVIDUAL SALVATION

In confronting the Augustinian approach to Paulinism that has dominated Western theology since the fifth century, N. T. Wright claims that a Copernican revolution is necessary to shift the focus from individual salvation to God's redemptive act for creation. Wright claims:

> The theological equivalent of supposing that the sun goes round the earth is the belief that the whole of Christian truth is all about me and my salvation. I have read dozens of books and articles . . . on the topic of justification. Again and again the writers, from a variety of backgrounds, have assumed, taken it for granted, that the central question of all is, "What must I do to be saved?" or (Luther's way of putting it), "How can I find a gracious God?" or, "How can I enter a right relationship with God?"[3]

For Wright, this displaces the central message of the Bible, which is that through humanity God could "bring his wise, glad, fruitful order to the world."[4]

While Justin is certainly no modern individualist (nor is Luther for that matter) who places his own salvation over his concern for the problems in the world, he does give primacy to the final destination of human beings over the Christian's work on the earth before death, and God's

3. Wright, *Justification*, 23.
4. Ibid.

## Justin Martyr

purposes for creation as a whole. While salvation is cosmic, its center is the salvation of sinful human beings. In a statement characteristic of his thought, Justin writes:

> Since those who did that which is universally, naturally, and eternally good are pleasing to God, they shall be saved through this Christ in the resurrection equally with those righteous men who were before them, namely Noah, and Enoch, and Jacob, and whoever else there be, along with those who have known this Christ, Son of God, who was before the morning star and the moon, and submitted to become incarnate, and be born of this virgin of the family of David, in order that, by this dispensation, the serpent that sinned from the beginning, and the angels like him, may be destroyed, and that death may be contemned, and forever quit, at the second coming of the Christ Himself, those who believe in Him and live acceptably,—and be no more: when some are sent to be punished unceasingly into judgment and condemnation of fire; but others shall exist in freedom from suffering, from corruption, and from grief, and in immortality."[5]

The main aspects of Justin's theology of redemption are present here. Salvation is viewed primarily as "immortality" and escaping the "condemnation of fire" that is prepared for the devil, his angels, and those who live wickedly. This salvation is achieved through faith in Christ, and maintained through virtuous living.

This focus on individual salvation is apparent throughout Justin's writings. In the beginning of his first apology, Justin articulates the reason Christians will not deny their faith in the face of persecution as to obtain the "eternal and

5. Justin, *Dial.* 45.

pure life"[6] with God. Justin opposes this to the fate of the wicked that will "undergo everlasting punishment."[7] Soon thereafter, discussing the resurrection, he warns that "Hell is a place where those are to be punished who have lived wickedly."[8] Again he adds, "We have learned that those only are deified who have lived near to God in holiness and virtue; and we believe that those who live wickedly and do not repent are punished in everlasting fire."[9] He writes that unbelievers will "be punished for an endless duration,"[10] while others will be "saved by repentance."[11] Christians are baptized so that they may be "saved with an everlasting salvation."[12] Finally, Justin concludes his apology with the following admonition: "For we forewarn you, that you shall not escape the coming judgment of God, if you continue in your injustice; and we ourselves will invite you to do that which is pleasing to God."[13]

Justin's other writings contain similar admonitions. In his second apology, he warns that "There shall be punishment in eternal fire inflicted upon those who do not live temperately and conformably to right reason."[14] Justin defends free will against Stoic philosophy, because only with free will can man "justly suffer in eternal fire."[15] In his *Dialogue with Trypho* Justin expresses his hope that Trypho

---

6. Justin, 1 *Apol.* 8.
7. Ibid.
8. Ibid., 19.
9. Ibid., 21.
10. Ibid., 28.
11. Ibid.
12. Ibid., 65.
13. Ibid., 67.
14. Justin, 2 *Apol.* 2.
15. Ibid., 7.

*Justin Martyr*

is among those who receive "the eternal salvation."[16] Justin prays that Trypho, by "believing on [Christ], may be saved in His second glorious advent, and may not be condemned to fire by Him."[17]

Justin assures Trypho that God "shall raise all men from the dead, and appoint some to be incorruptible, immortal, and free from sorrow in the everlasting and imperishable kingdom; but shall send others away to the everlasting punishment of fire."[18] These quotes are interspersed throughout Justin's writings, along with several others that could be cited. A thorough reading of Justin's writings makes his concern for individual salvation apparent.

In light of the evidence, it is untenable to suggest that the question "What must I do to be saved?" was not a predominant question at this time in the early church. While Justin likely did not theologize about the connection between faith and works in ones justification, he can hardly speak of a topic without mentioning the "eternal fire" he expects those who persecute Christians and live wickedly to suffer, and the blessings of immortal life for Christians and righteous philosophers.

Even moral living is secondary to the topic of salvation.[19] While Justin, belonging to the Greek philosophical tradition, is concerned with virtuous living and a temperate life, he does not discuss ethics with a view to establishing "happiness" in the Aristotelian sense. Nor does he limit virtuous living to the select few—the philosophers. For Justin,

16. Justin, *Dial.* 32.
17. Ibid., 35.
18. Ibid., 117.
19. "And we have learned that those only are deified who have lived near to God in holiness and virtue; and we believe that those who live wickedly and do not repent are punished in everlasting fire" (Justin, 1 *Apol.* 21).

## The Righteousness of One

virtuous living is of a subsidiary value. It is merely a stepping stone on the path to eternal salvation. One lives the virtuous life to escape being "condemned to fire by Him."[20]

In light of Alister McGrath's appraisal of Justin as a more thorough Platonist than Pauline Christian,[21] it may be objected that Justin's soteriological focus is due not to the influence of Paulinism in his thought but to an exposition of Plato's view of the afterlife. Perhaps the Pauline view is of a universal recreation, and Justin—due to his middle Platonism—ignores the physical nature of redemption in favor of the salvation of an immaterial soul. This, however, does not do justice to Justin's own words. While Justin is willing to admit similarities between his views and those of Greek philosophy,[22] he explicitly rejects a spirit/matter dualism. Salvation is a matter of the whole man, not an escape from physicality:

> For if you have fallen in with some who are called Christians, but who do not admit this [truth], and venture to blaspheme the God of Abraham, and the God of Isaac, and the God of Jacob; who say there is no resurrection of the dead, and that their souls, when they die, are taken to heaven; do not imagine that they

---

20. Justin, *Dial.* 35.

21. McGrath, *Iustitia Dei*, 34–36. McGrath does not go as far as Harnack in this respect.

22. "[W]hile we say that there will be a burning up of all, we shall seem to utter the doctrine of the Stoics: and while we affirm that the souls of the wicked, being endowed with sensation even after death, are punished, and that those of the good being delivered from punishment spend a blessed existence, we shall seem to say the same things as the poets and philosophers; and while we maintain that men ought not to worship the works of their hands, we say the very things which have been said by the comic poet Menander, and other similar writers, for they have declared that the workman is greater than the work" (Justin, 1 *Apol.* 20).

*Justin Martyr*

are Christians, even as one, if he would rightly consider it, would not admit that the Sadducees, or similar sects of Genistæ, Meristæ, Galilæans, Hellenists, Pharisees, Baptists, are Jews (do not hear me impatiently when I tell you what I think), but are [only] called Jews and children of Abraham, worshipping God with the lips, as God Himself declared, but the heart was far from Him. But I and others, who are right-minded Christians on all points, are assured that there will be a resurrection of the dead, and a thousand years in Jerusalem, which will then be built, adorned, and enlarged, [as] the prophets Ezekiel and Isaiah and others declare.[23]

Justin argues that the soul itself does not constitute a man, nor does a soulless body. He compares the body-soul unity to an oxen and a yolk. As an oxen and a yolk cannot plow except together, the body and soul cannot work except as a unit.[24]

I propose that the reason Justin focuses on the destiny of individuals, rather than the Christian's duty to social action, or even the virtuous life, is a thoroughly Christian one, untainted by Greek philosophy. As his name testifies, Justin lived and wrote in an age of persecutions and martyrdom. This being the case, Justin's focus was pointed toward the end result of this martyrdom: life after death. Justin writes, "And if you also read these words in a hostile spirit, ye can do no more, as I said before, than kill us; which indeed does no harm to us, but to you and all who unjustly hate us, and do not repent, brings eternal punishment by

---

23. Justin, *Dial.* 80.

24. "For as in the case of a yoke of oxen, if one or other is loosed from the yoke, neither of them can plough alone; so neither can soul or body alone effect anything, if they be unyoked from their communion" (Justin, *On the Resurrection* 13).

fire."²⁵ Justin's soteriology is often placed in this context of the persecuted and the persecutor. The persecuted receives eternal life, while the persecutor receives eternal damnation. In a time when Christians were regularly put to death, the question of salvation was perhaps even more pertinent than in sixteenth-century Europe. Christians did not have the luxury to focus on their duty to social action and restoring the world.

## FAITH AND WORKS

While it is evident that Justin asked the Lutheran/Augustinian question of how one can be saved from condemnation, Justin's answer is less clear. Does Justin point to the imputed and sufficient righteousness of Christ as opposed to man's active righteousness as Luther would? Well, no—not exactly. If one is expecting to find the clarity of an exposition of the work of Christ as in the *Epistle to Diognetus*,²⁶ he will be thoroughly disappointed. Justin often, especially in his *First Apology*, argues that virtue is the path to salvation. However, there is another strand of a thoroughly christological understanding of salvation that surfaces from time to time in Justin's writings.

Some have argued for a Reformational reading of Justin. Nick Needham argues that Justin teaches a "bold doctrine of imputed righteousness."²⁷ This thesis can hardly be substantiated. To defend this statement, Needham cites Justin's comments on Ezekiel in his dialogue with Trypho:

---

25. Justin, 1 *Apol.* 45.

26. This is one of the many reasons that the Justinian authorship of *Diognetus* is untenable.

27. Needham, "Justification in the Early Church Fathers," 32.

*Justin Martyr*

> For the goodness and loving-kindness of God, and His boundless riches, hold righteous and sinless the person who, as Ezekiel tells, repents of sins; and reckons sinful, unrighteous, and impious the person who falls away from piety and righteousness to unrighteousness and ungodliness.[28]

In context, Justin is writing to Trypho about those Christians who obey the Mosaic law. While Justin admits the probable salvation of those who obey the law without imposing this burden on others, he warns Trypho that both Judaizing Christians who view obedience to Moses as a necessity and unrepentant Jews will not escape punishment from God. The statement cited by Needham serves not as an admonition to trust in the imputed righteousness of Christ, but a warning that the unrepentance of Jews before death results in condemnation.

There is no contextual reason to assume that Justin argues for justification of the ungodly. In the second part of the quote, Justin argues that God holds "unrighteous, and impious" those who have fallen from the Christian way of life to one that is full of "unrighteousness and ungodliness." In other words, God's reckoning merely establishes that which is already true. It is likely that Justin is making a consistent parallel wherein those who are reckoned righteous actually *are* righteous and sinless through repentance. This would be consistent with Justin's manner of speaking elsewhere: "If, indeed, you repent of your sins, and recognize Him to be Christ, and observe His commandments . . . remission of sins shall be yours."[29] Though the quote cited by Needham emphasizes the reality of forgiveness, and Justin's

---

28. Justin, *Dial.* 47.
29. Ibid., 95.

## The Righteousness of One

belief in the mercy of God, Justin is far from teaching justification by alien righteousness.

Justin can state rather bluntly that "Each man goes to everlasting punishment or salvation according to the value of his actions."[30] On this point, Justin could not be farther from Luther. Rather than justification of the ungodly, Justin argues that only those who are worthy of grace receive salvation.[31] Justin speaks of two kinds of righteousness as does Luther; however, rather than speaking of active and passive righteousness, or self-righteousness and alien righteousness, he speaks of love of God and love of neighbor. Observance of these two commandments makes one righteous.[32] As if directly refuting the concept of alien righteousness, Justin declares that "Each one . . . shall be saved by his own righteousness."[33] In light of these comments, Justin appears as a proto-Pelagian.

Justin does not, however, negate the importance of personal faith in one's salvation. For example, he can state that one through "believing on Him [Christ], may be saved in His second glorious advent, and may not be condemned to fire by Him."[34] He writes that "[All] who believe in Christ, and recognize the truth in His own words and those of His prophets, know that they shall be with Him in that

---

30. Justin, 1 *Apol.* 12.

31. "if men by their works show themselves worthy of this His design, they are deemed worthy, and so we have received—of reigning in company with Him, being delivered from corruption and suffering." First Apology X

32. "Therefore, since all righteousness is divided into two branches, namely, in so far as it regards God and men, whoever, says the Scripture, loves the Lord God with all the heart, and all the strength, and his neighbour as himself, would be truly a righteous man" (Justin, *Dial.* 92).

33. Ibid., 45.

34. Ibid., 35.

## Justin Martyr

land, and inherit everlasting and incorruptible good." One's faith is often connected with the work of Christ, and with baptism. Making a parallel to Noah's salvation in the ark, Justin writes that "By water, faith, and wood, those who are afore-prepared, and who repent of the sins which they have committed, shall escape from the impending judgment of God."[35] Justin's soteriology is one that gives efficacy to both faith and works regarding one's salvation.

There is a strand in Justin's teaching that emphasizes God's grace and forgiveness. God is not a harsh judge, but he "desires rather the repentance than the punishment of the sinner."[36] God give repentance as a remedy from man's enslavement to evil. All who repent "escape their sins."[37] Repentance for Justin is always connected to the sacramental act of baptism. One receives in baptism "the remission of sins formerly committed."[38] This baptism is given to one "who chooses to be born again, and has repented of his sins." Justin calls this the "water of life"[39] for those are believers in Christ. Though Justin gives efficacy to baptism as a saving act on behalf of sinners, he does not treat the issue of post-baptismal sins. Does baptism merely forgive past sins, or is it a protection against future sins and a continual source of grace? Unfortunately, this question remains unanswered. Justin's writings are inconclusive.

35. Ibid., 138.
36. Justin, 1 *Apol.* 15.
37. Ibid., 61.
38. Ibid.
39. Ibid., 14.

The Righteousness of One

## THE LAW

One of the central challenges to the "Lutheran" reading of Paul by NPP proponents is that Luther misunderstood the Pauline use of the term νομος. For the NPP, the law belongs to the Mosaic legislation, and does not require perfect obedience. However, for Luther and the Reformation, "law" in Paul's polemics refers to good works in general, and requires perfect obedience. If one does not obey the law completely, he is placed under its curse only to be freed by the grace of God in Christ. While Justin is not willing to broaden the term "law" as far as Luther, he does anticipate his understanding of obedience. For Justin, the law requires perfection, and no one living has achieved this perfection. Therefore, all are under the law's curse, and need to be rescued by an outside source.[40]

In his most extensive treatment on the subject, Justin writes:

> "For the whole human race will be found to be under a curse. For it is written in the law of Moses, 'Cursed is every one that continueth not in all things that are written in the book of the law to do them.' And no one has accurately done all, nor will you venture to deny this; but some more and some less than others have observed the ordinances enjoined. But if those who are under this law appear to be under a curse for not having observed all the requirements, how much more shall all the nations appear to be under a curse who practise idolatry, who seduce youths, and commit other crimes? If, then, the Father of all wished His Christ for the whole human

---

40. An in-depth examination of Justin's view of the law, specifically in analyzing his division of the between moral and ceremonial, is in Stylianopoulos, *Justin Martyr and the Mosaic Law*.

*Justin Martyr*

> family to take upon Him the curses of all, knowing that, after He had been crucified and was dead, He would raise Him up, why do you argue about Him, who submitted to suffer these things according to the Father's will, as if He were accursed, and do not rather bewail yourselves? For although His Father caused Him to suffer these things in behalf of the human family, yet you did not commit the deed as in obedience to the will of God. For you did not practise piety when you slew the prophets. And let none of you say: If His Father wished Him to suffer this, in order that by His stripes the human race might be healed, we have done no wrong. If, indeed, you repent of your sins, and recognise Him to be Christ, and observe His commandments, then you may assert this; for, as I have said before, remission of sins shall be yours. But if you curse Him and them that believe on Him, and, when you have the power, put them to death, how is it possible that requisition shall not be made of you, as of unrighteous and sinful men, altogether hardhearted and without understanding because you laid your hands on him?[41]

Justin relates this curse to "all human beings." Therefore, the Pauline discussion of law is necessarily broader than the Mosaic legislation given to Israel. All of humanity, at least in some sense, owes obedience to the law.

Justin interprets the extensive nature of Paul's citation of Deuteronomy 27:26 in the same manner as Luther, not the NPP. According to E. P. Sanders, the term "all" in Paul's citation is irrelevant to his argument. Paul desired to equate "curse" with the "law," and thus found a corresponding text. The exact terminology of Deuteronomy was

41. Justin, *Dial.* 95.

merely incidental.⁴² Justin, however, emphasizes that "No one has accurately done *all*" that is commanded in the law (emphasis mine). He then states that one must observe "*all* the requirements" (emphasis mine). Justin's words merit the conclusion that he believed the law to require perfect, not partial, obedience.

Justin also emphasizes that no one has been able to keep the whole law. He states bluntly that "No one has accurately done all." This is not limited to the nation of Israel, but applies to "all the nations . . . who practice idolatry." Paul's argument in Galatians 3, therefore, does not refer to Israel's exile, but to the plight of disobedient mankind. The law requires perfect obedience from all, and none have fulfilled its ordinances. Luther's primary use of the law, therefore, has precedence in Justin's theology.

Because of this disobedience, all are "worthy of a curse."⁴³ Both Israel and the surrounding nations "appear to be under a curse."⁴⁴ Though these statements may give the impression that humanity is not truly under God's curse but only appear to be, and deserve to be, Justin clearly states that "The whole human race" *is* "under a curse."⁴⁵ A divine rescue is necessary from the plight all mankind has incurred through disobedience to God's law.

## CHRIST IN JUSTIN'S SOTERIOLOGY

As was stated above, Justin's soteriology, as philosophically influenced as it may be, is thoroughly christological. Christ

---

42. This comes from Sanders belief that Paul argued from solution to plight, thus several inconsistencies exist in his view of sin and the law.

43. Justin, *Dial.* 94.

44. Ibid., 95.

45. Ibid.

## Justin Martyr

is not placed on the level of other philosophers, nor is he viewed as the best of all philosophers. Contrary to some other philosophically minded church fathers, Justin views Christ's life, death, and resurrection as salvific acts greater than the wisdom he displayed in his teaching. Justin is far from transforming the Christian message into a vague moralism.

The cross is the central event in redemptive history. Justin tirelessly makes parallels between Old Testament narratives and phrases and the cross. The red string that Rahab uses to save Israel's spies, the animal sacrifices, the ark, and the bronze serpent are all pictures of Israel's Messiah, and his death.

The cross brings salvation to Christians. Those who believe in him are cleansed by his blood.[46] He partook of our sufferings that "He might also bring us healing."[47] Christ redeemed mankind "by being crucified on the tree, and by purifying [us] with water."[48] Through the blood of Christ, "persons out of all nations are saved, receiving remission of sins, and continuing no longer in sin."[49] This cross-centered approach to theology permeates Justin's writings.

That the cross is essential is obvious in Justin, but the question remains of Justin's atonement theory. Does he utilize one? One should not expect to find a full-blown exposition of penal substitution, Anselmian satisfaction, or any other elaborate atonement theory. Justin's works are of an apologetic nature, and do not present a systematic

---

46. "For this 'washing His robe in the blood of the grape' was predictive of the passion He was to endure, cleansing by His blood those who believe on Him" (Justin, 1 Apol. 33).

47. Ibid., 13.

48. Justin, *Dial.* 86.

49. Ibid., 111.

treatment of atonement. Likely, Justin's thought ran deeper than is apparent in his surviving works; however, his view of the cross must be evaluated from the occasional references he makes to his teaching on the matter.

Some have argued that Justin teaches an early doctrine of penal substitution,[50] wherein God pours out his wrath on Christ in place of humanity. The defense of this concept comes from a solitary quote from his *Dialogue with Trypho*:

> If, then, the Father of all wished His Christ for the whole human family to take upon Him the curses of all, knowing that, after He had been crucified and was dead, He would raise Him up, why do you argue about Him, who submitted to suffer these things according to the Father's will, as if He were accursed, and do not rather bewail yourselves?[51]

The assumption of penal substitution arises from Justin's use of the phrase "take upon Him the curses of all" in reference to Christ's death. There is however, no language of God's wrath, or Christ taking another's punishment. While this would be consistent with Justin's language, it is not necessitated by it.

Justin does use Paul's concept in Galatians 3:13 of Christ taking away the curses of those under the law—a prominent theme in Luther. However, this is not meant in an entirely Lutheran manner as is apparent in his discussion of the curse. Justin does not, as Paul and Luther do, propose that Christ placed himself under the curse of the law. On the contrary, Justin uses the same verse as Paul (Deuteronomy 21:23) to defend a different thesis: Moses, while writing Deuteronomy, prophesied the rejection of

50. This claim is made in Jeffery, *Pierced for Our Transgressions*.
51. Justin, *Dial.* 95.

## Justin Martyr

Christ within Judaism, and subsequently Jews cursing the Messiah. This is the "curse" that Christ is under. As the holy Son of God, Christ cannot truly be under a curse, but is accused of being so by unrepentant Jews. Justin explicitly states that it is not that "He who has been crucified is cursed by God."[52] Justin is far from Pauline in this argument.

The above statement and that which has been used to defend penal substitution must be harmonized. Justin can at once state both that Christ takes "upon Him the curses of all"[53] and that Christ is not "cursed by God."[54] It seems that the cross, for Justin, takes away the curse that all men are under for disobeying God's law. On this ground, Justin is thoroughly consistent with a Lutheran understanding of the law and atonement. However, Justin does not go so far as to admit that Christ took away this curse by placing himself under it. There must be another means of atonement in Justin's theology: the resurrection.

Perhaps the reason that Justin has been described as a moralist who lacked understanding of the New Testament gospel is due to the neglect of resurrection in much of Western theology. If the cross is not mentioned apart from the incarnation and resurrection as a saving force, then one is assumed to miss the Pauline message. This however, is far from both the New Testament message, and from Luther's theology. The cross's efficacy only reaches its fulfillment through Christ, the firstborn of the resurrection, and subsequently man's participation in this resurrection life through the sacraments.

For Justin, Christ "endured both to be set at nought and to suffer, that by dying and rising again He might

---

52. Ibid., 96.
53. Ibid., 95.
54. Ibid., 96.

conquer death."⁵⁵ Along with many other patristic writers, Justin views death as a foe that needs to be vanquished. Christ must partake of death in order to rise and defeat the enemy. This death and corruption is the chief result of Adam's sin. God proposed that if Adam would obey his commands, he would "partake of immortal existence; but if he transgressed it, the contrary should be his lot. Man having been thus made, and immediately looking towards transgression, naturally became subject to corruption."⁵⁶ Thus Christ partakes of humanity in order to suffer Adam's lot, and return immortality to mankind through the resurrection. Though perhaps inconsistent with the later protestant tradition, this strand of resurrection theology is prominent throughout Luther's writings, as is evidenced above.

## THEOSIS

Though Justin is more philosophically oriented than Irenaeus, he does not cease to utilize several of the same soteriological concepts. He anticipates recapitulation, though it does not receive that full treatment that it does in Irenaeus.⁵⁷ Justin teaches, as Luther, a robust doctrine of incarnation, whereby through Christ humanity partakes of immortality and salvation. Only through Christ's two natures, as God and man, can fellowship between God and sinful man be restored.

Christ was made "Man by a virgin, according to the counsel of the Father, for the salvation of those who believe

---

55. Justin, 1 *Apol.* 63.

56. Justin, Fragment 11.

57. Irenaeus himself cites Justin Martyr in reference to recapitulation. Irenaeus, *Against Heresies* 4.6.1.

## Justin Martyr

on Him."[58] For Justin, Christ's incarnation, life, death, and resurrection are necessary to restore life to mankind. Christ "became man for our sakes."[59] Through the incarnation, Christ did not merely become a singular man, but participated in humanity as a whole. In dying as a man, healing was brought about for all men. In his lost work on the resurrection, Justin rhetorically asks, "If He had no need of the flesh, why did He heal it?"[60] Justin implies that healing of man's flesh occurs through Christ's participation in it.

Justin's clearest statement on the issue comes from a lost writing quoted by Leontius:

> For He ordained that, if he kept this, he should partake of immortal existence; but if he transgressed it, the contrary should be his lot. Man having been thus made, and immediately looking towards transgression, naturally became subject to corruption. Corruption then becoming inherent in nature, it was necessary that He who wished to save should be one who destroyed the efficient cause of corruption. And this could not otherwise be done than by the life which is according to nature being united to that which had received the corruption, and so destroying the corruption, while preserving as immortal for the future that which had received it. It was therefore necessary that the Word should become possessed of a body, that He might deliver us from the death of natural corruption. For if, as ye say, He had simply by a nod warded off death from us, death indeed would not have approached us on account of the expression of His

---

58. Justin, 1 *Apol.* 63.

59. Ibid., 13.

60. *Lost Treatise on the Resurrection* IX. Whether or not this work is genuine, the sentiment is Justinian.

## The Righteousness of One

> will; but none the less would we again have become corruptible, inasmuch as we carried about in ourselves that natural corruption.[61]

Justin once again gives primacy to the incarnation. Man participates in divinity through Christ's participation in manhood. In his death, Christ unites himself to the defeat all men face, and through his resurrection conquers it for all who follow him. Luther follows Justin on this point rather closely.

Justin's notion of *theosis* is a prominent theme in his Eucharistic theology. The wine and bread in the eucharistic celebration are not "common bread and common drink,"[62] but are the very body and blood of Christ. When one partakes of the Eucharist, a *communicatio idiomatum* takes place. The body and blood of the participant in communion are changed by "transmutation."[63] That which properly belongs to Christ is given to those who feed on him in bread and wine. Attributes of Christ are transferred to the believer. This only occurs because it is the "flesh and blood of that Jesus who was made flesh."[64] There is a "great exchange" in Justin whereby Christ takes upon himself a human nature and places himself under the burden of death; subsequently Christ conquers death on behalf of mankind and transforms man by participation in him through faith. That which belongs to man is taken by Christ, and that which belongs to Christ is gifted to man by grace. This is the framework wherein Luther's doctrine of imputation is formulated.

---

61. Leontius, *Against the Eutychians*, book 2, frag. XI.
62. Justin, 1 *Apol.* 66.
63. Ibid.
64. Ibid.

## CONCLUSION

Justin has been shown to anticipate Luther's understanding of Paul in various ways. First, Justin is concerned with the salvation of individual souls. The question "What must I do to be saved?" is one that Justin both asked and answered. This is a pertinent question in the human existential situation, not merely a concern of the late Middle Ages. The real motive behind asking the question is a simple one: the reality of death. This was a great reality in the first three centuries of the church due to ongoing persecution, which eventually took Justin's life.

Justin also approaches Luther's understanding of God's law. This law is universal, and condemns all under its curse. This curse is not connected to Israel's exile. The law does not require partial, but total, obedience. Since all have sinned, the law does not save. Christ died on behalf of the curse all are under. Justin does not admit, however, that Christ himself is placed under the curse, as is Luther's view.

There are several differences between the two theologians. Luther believes in salvation *sola fide*, whereas Justin views both faith and works as efficacious. Justin does not posit alien righteousness, but one's own righteousness as a saving force. Love of God and love of neighbor are effects of God's saving act in Luther, but in Justin they are both effects of past grace and a cause of future grace.

There is, however, significant agreement in one aspect of Luther's doctrine of justification. For both figures, salvation comes through a union of God and man. This union was affected in the incarnation, and approaches man through faith and the sacraments. In baptism one receives forgiveness, and through the Eucharist he receives Christ and is gradually brought into greater union with God. There is a sharing between Christ and the believer wherein that which belongs to the Christian is given to Christ, and that which is Christ's is given to the believer. If this is the groundwork wherein Luther's understanding of double imputation is formulated, Justin is not far from a "Lutheran" understanding of salvation.

Wright's reading of Paul is unknown to Justin. Perhaps this is due to the fact that Justin's Platonism influenced his hermeneutics, blinding him to Paul's intended meaning. Or perhaps Justin's understanding is closer to that of the first-century churches to which Paul was writing. These churches were concerned with the salvation of individual men and women of whom death had taken a hold through the law's curse.

# 7

# Conclusion

Now that the texts have been analyzed, some conclusions can be drawn regarding Pauline interpretation in the early church. There is by no means a unanimous consensus in all of the fathers examined; however all four of these figures have certain strains of thought that comport with Luther's Paulinism and diverge from that of the NPP proponents. Now each topic that is central to the NPP debate can be analyzed.

## JUSTIFICATION

Though there is no unanimous consensus on the definition of justification for the proponents of the NPP, there are several points of contact between the four major writers analyzed in this study. First, justification is not used by Paul in the context that it is for Luther and the Reformation tradition; it does not answer the problem of a tormented conscience. There is no law/gospel background for Paul's use of justification. It is meant to answer the question of table fellowship. The problem Paul was responding to, according to Wright, was not about soteriology, but ecclesiology.[1] As Wright defines the term, "Justification in Galatians, is the doctrine which insists that all who share faith in Christ belong to the same table, no matter what their racial differences, as together they wait for the final creation."[2] In other words, justification identifies one as a member of the covenant, but does not bring one into the covenant.

Another aspect of the NPP that purports to overthrow the Reformation understanding of Paul is a denial of imputation. According to these interpreters, the Lutheran view states that God gives the righteousness of himself, or of Christ, to the believer and consequently judges him as righteous. There is nothing transformational about righteousness; it is a bare covering. This, all four of the aforementioned interpreters are found to be in error. Paul posits righteousness, at least according to Wright, as God's covenant faithfulness. It can't be given or transferred to another. This is a confusion of categories, and flows from late medieval debates foreign to the Pauline material. Since Luther, and in some ways Augustine, the explication of the concept of God's righteousness has been misapplied.

Most of the NPP authors apply a type of covenantal nomism to the Apostle Paul's teaching. One is a member of the covenant by grace, and then this status must be maintained through faithful living. The Lutheran concepts of *sola fide* and *simul iustus et peccator* are to be rejected as inaccurate renderings of Paulinism. For Luther, justification involves the forgiveness of sins, and the giving of a new heart. As Luther defines the term in the Smalcald Articles,

---

1. "In standard Christian theological language, [Justification] wasn't so much about soteriology as about ecclesiology; not so much about salvation as about the church" (Wright, What Saint Paul Really Said, 119).

2. Ibid., 22.

*Conclusion*

"Through faith we have a new and clean heart, and God will and does account us entirely righteous and holy for the sake of Christ our Mediator."[3] The question that Paul is answering is that of the universal sinfulness of mankind. Paul's polemic against Jewish works is primarily regarding soteriology.[4] "How must I be saved?" is the primary question interpreters should be asking when approaching Paul's epistle to the Romans.

Luther affirms the imputation of Christ's righteousness to the believer. However, the caricature of this view has been shown to be mistaken. For Luther, righteousness is not a mere attribute that can be passed from a judge to a guilty defendant. The believer, through faith, receives Christ. This same Christ, who lived, died, and was raised on the Christian's behalf, then becomes the Christian's righteousness. The believer is righteous, not by a legal transaction in the heavenly courts, but because the believer and his savior become united in a marriage bond through faith. There is then a *communicatio idiomatum* in which the Christian receives that which belongs properly to Christ, and Christ takes the Christian's sin upon himself.

Finally, for Luther, justification is the result of faith alone. Only faith can receive Christ and his benefits. When one is united to Christ through faith, he remains a sinner, but is counted wholly righteous for the sake of Jesus. His old self is entirely sinful, but Christ, who is united to the sinner, is entirely righteous.

Clement propounds the concept of justification in a manner similar to Luther,

---

3. Smalcald Articles 3.13.1.

4. Luther does not only view the Pauline epistles as discussing soteriology. A look at the controversial work *On the Jews and their Lies* demonstrates that identification in God's community is as an essential aspect of Pauline theology for Luther as well.

> And so we, having been called through his will in Christ Jesus, are not justified through themselves or their own works or the righteous actions that they did, but through his will. And so we, having been called through his will in Christ Jesus, are not justified through ourselves or our own wisdom or understanding or piety, or works that we have done in holiness of heart, but through faith, by which the Almighty God has justified all who have existed from the beginning; to whom be the glory for ever and ever. Amen.[5]

It was demonstrated above that for Clement justification is a soteriological term. It does not identify one as a member of God's covenant people in the context of table fellowship and Jew-Gentile relations. It is answering the question of good works before God, not marks of identification among Christians. Faith receives soteriological benefits, and is not a badge of covenant membership. It was also made apparent that for Clement man is justified *sola fide*. Whether or not an imputation occurs that causes justification is unclear in Clement. What is clear, however, is that one's own righteousness does not justify, but the work of another. Clement's view of justification comports with the Lutheran understanding, not the NPP.

Ignatius uses the term "justification" twice, and it is unclear exactly how Ignatius uses the term. The most explicit reference to the subject is as follows: "But for me, the 'archives' are Jesus Christ, the unalterable archives are his cross and death and his resurrection and the faith that comes through him; by these things I want, through your prayers, to be justified."[6] Due to the connection of justifi-

---

5. *1 Clem.* 32:3–4.
6. Ignatius, *Phld.* 8:2.

*Conclusion*

cation and resurrection here, as well as parallel passages, it seems that justification is connected with eschatology and is attached to one's resurrection. This eschatological focus is an agreement with both Luther and Wright. The three instrumental causes of justification, for Ignatius, are Christ's death, resurrection, and faith. Faith thus is a means of receiving eschatological salvation through Christ's work, not a badge of covenant membership.

It was established that *sola fide* is not inconsistent with Ignatian theology, as he consistently emphasizes faith in soteriological contexts, and never attributes justification to works. However, Ignatius' writings do not have the clarity for a definitive declaration on the subject.

Regarding imputation, there is no clear evidence that Ignatius directly taught the concept. However, Ignatian mysticism lends itself to Luther's explication of the concept. This is apparent in his ecclesiological discussion in which Ignatius posits a real participation in God through corporate worship. This participation in God comes to its zenith as one receives Christ in the Eucharist, nurturing one unto eternal life. Luther's concept of imputation occurs within this common framework.

For the *Epistle to Diognetus*, justification is a soteriological term. It answers the question of man's inability to enter the kingdom of God through his own works. There is nothing in his discussion of the subject about covenant identification or table fellowship. Soteriology is central, not ecclesiology. He describes it as a response to man's sin, and as a result of God's mercy in Christ. The context of the doctrine of justification for the author of *Diognetus* and Luther is nearly identical.

Faith is the means of receiving justification for the author of *Diognetus*. The only mention of works in context is their inability to achieve righteousness and allow one to enter the kingdom of God. While *Diognetus* does not specify the role of works after conversion, what he states regarding the issue comports with Luther's doctrine of *sola fide*.

The author of *Diognetus*, unlike the other fathers, explicitly teaches a doctrine of imputation. He regards the righteousness of God, not as God's covenant faithfulness, but as the righteousness of Christ.[7] There is a great exchange between the believer and his savior, as Christ freely takes man's sin upon himself and consequently gives himself as righteousness to the Christian. Nearly every attack the NPP proponents throw at Luther could be applied to *Diognetus* as well.

Finally, Justin Martyr also views the Pauline polemic as a plea for individual salvation. Justin does not address the issue of covenant identification, but consistently emphasizes the reality of hell and the need for personal faith in Christ for eternal life. The central aspect of the Christian faith, for Justin, is eternal life with God, which he constantly presents to his readers.

There is clear evidence in Justin's writings that he does not hold to *sola fide* as is taught in Luther, Clement, and *Diognetus*. He consistently writes of works as efficacious. They are not mere evidence of saving faith, but cause one to be righteous before God. Rather than imputation, Justin posits that one's own righteousness is the garment that God will look upon to evaluate man's worthiness to enter his kingdom.

However, Justin does agree with Luther's view of union with Christ, which has been ignored by NPP proponents. He approaches Irenaeus' concept of recapitulation by

---

7. An exegetical critique of Wright's definition of righteousness can be found in Seifrid, "Righteousness Language in the Hebrew Scriptures." Seifrid demonstrates that in the Hebrew scriptures the terms "righteousness" and "covenant" barely come into any significant semantic contact.

## Conclusion

teaching that incorruption must be united to corruption so that man may be saved. Christ, the immortal God, becomes mortal man and dies in order to take upon himself that which belongs to fallen creation. In turn, Christ gives what is proper to deity to the believer who has been baptized. There is a *communicatio idiomatum*, as there is in Luther, between Christ and his people. This is nourished through participation in the Eucharist, as it is in Ignatius. Though imputation is denied by Justin, he shares the presuppositions which the concept is built upon.

All four patristic sources agree with Luther that the doctrine of justification belongs in a soteriological rather than ecclesiological[8] context. Both Clement and Diognetus teach *sola fide*, and Ignatius at least approaches the concept. Justin, however, denies it. The author of *Diognetus* explicitly teaches imputation, and the necessary backdrop for Luther's formulation of the doctrine is propounded in Ignatius and Justin. *Diognetus* explicitly rejects Wright's identification of the righteousness of God with his covenant faithfulness, and identifies it with that of Christ.

## THE LAW

For the NPP, the law in Paulinism primarily refers to Jewish identity. It does not refer to good works in general, which condemn all men, as the Reformation tradition has taught. As Stendahl purports, Paul does not write about the insufficiency of the law because of its impossibility to fulfill perfectly, but simply because the law is not Christ. Paul did not have a law/gospel concept as did later Lutheranism, in teaching that one must first be slain by the law, see his insufficiency and wickedness before God, and then receive

8. This is not to say that it does not have ecclesiological implications for these writers.

the gospel of grace by the all-sufficient work of Christ. According to Stendahl, the opposite is the case; Paul sees that Christ is the true way of salvation. Therefore, all other means, including the law, are insufficient. The argument is from solution to plight, not plight to solution.[9]

The other NPP proponents do not necessarily agree with Stendahl's total analysis here, but all concur that the Lutheran position is mistaken. The law does not require perfect obedience. Rather, the law requires a righteousness that is not Christian. This is why Paul does not promote law righteousness. It excludes Gentiles, and has become a tool of ethnic superiority used by ethnocentric Judaism. The law is a badge of membership in the covenant. However, it excludes Gentiles. Faith justifies all men because it is the true badge of membership in the new covenant, regardless of ethnic heritage. For Paul, the gospel is primarily about a universalistic conception of covenant membership, the message that *all* who have faith are Abraham's offspring; this is in contradistinction to the Lutheran emphasis that all who have *faith* are Abraham's offspring.

For the NPP, the law serves as a mark of Jewish identity. The law is not *any* command God gives to his people, but those that deal with the nation of Israel specifically. This is why the subject of circumcision and food laws are the central aspects of law discussed and the book of Galatians. Paul's polemic is over the issue of table fellowship, not eternal salvation.

For Luther, the law requires perfect obedience. The law calls for that which is impossible; primarily the total love of God, and submission to his will above all else. In essence, the first commandment must be obeyed. The law was not primarily given by God as a means to live in the covenant, to show humans how to be moral creatures, but

9. For an exegetical critique, see Thielman, *From Plight to Solution*.

*Conclusion*

to show men that they cannot fulfill it. The law is a hammer that smashes man's self-sufficiency, his attempts at self-justification, and his pride. Through the law, men come to see the reality that they are sinners. Not only have men disobeyed the law from time to time, but man's entire life is one of sin. Even his best works are seen as filthy rags before God.

For Luther, plight precedes solution. Law precedes gospel. One must first recognize and admit his sin before he will be able to hear and accept the gospel. Though the law does have something to do with ethnic identity, it primarily refers to moral commands. Whereas the NPP limits the usage of νομοσ to Torah, Luther uses a much more broad interpretation of the phrase. Law in essence means command.[10] It refers to any imperative given by God to humanity. Though Jewish laws such as those related to Sabbath keeping, circumcision, and purification are intended as law for Luther, this is not because law has a specific reference to ethnic identification, but because these rituals and regulations are categorized as "commands."

Luther and the NPP have fundamentally different concepts of the law. For the NPP, the law refers to Jewish identity markers, not commands in general. For Luther, law refers to any command given to God's people. For the NPP, the law is not impossible to fulfill but simply misses Christ. For Luther, the law is impossible to fulfill because it requires perfect obedience, which no man can render.

---

10. In a much neglected work, Vlachos, *Law and the Knowledge of Good and Evil*, the thesis is defended that because Paul identifies law as Edenic (i.e., Rom 5) it is a creational category rather than a Mosaic category in his thought. Since God's first command was broken by Adam and brought death, God's commands have done the same ever since. Thus a broader interpretation of law is not prominent only in Lutheran dogmatic theology, but in some Pauline scholarship as well.

## The Righteousness of One

Ignatius' seven epistles do not contain much information regarding his perspective on the law. Whether or not the law requires perfect obedience, and is a prerequisite for understanding the gospel, or is a mark of ethnic identity, is unclear. What is apparent is that soteriological concerns are central to Ignatius' thought.

In the *Epistle to Diognetus*, a "Lutheran" perspective is explicated. The author writes, first, of the situation of man's sin before God before he addresses God's remedy through the cross. As in Luther, law precedes gospel. *Diognetus* argues from plight to solution. Works can never earn merit before God, because they always fall short. According to *Diognetus*, we "were convicted by our own deeds as unworthy of life." The doctrine of justification answers the problems of man's own inability to enter the kingdom of God through his own merit. There is no indication in *Diognetus* that the law is limited to Mosaic law and ethnic exclusivism, but applies to good works in general, which show man his own impossibility of attaining salvation. One only enters the kingdom of God when he is "enabled to do so by God's power." The interpretation of the law proposed by the NPP is utterly foreign to the *Epistle to Diognetus*.

Justin Martyr likewise has been shown to hold to what would later be coined the "Lutheran" approach to the law. For Justin, the law requires perfection, as he cites Deuteronomy 27:26 to demonstrate. Justin believes likewise that the law is imposed as a standard that is impossible for mankind to fulfill. As Justin states, "No one has accurately done all."[11] This does not include only the nation of Israel, which the NPP would advocate limiting "law" to the Mosaic law given to Israel. It applies to "the whole human race."[12] The fact that none have obeyed the law perfectly results in a

11. Justin, *Dial.* 95.
12. Ibid.

*Conclusion*

curse over all of mankind. A divine rescue is necessary that this curse may be lifted. This curse is then lifted by Christ.[13] This curse is not the exile, as is argued by Wright.[14]

Luther's approach to the law is vindicated as thoroughly patristic by three of the above-mentioned writers.[15] Clement, Justin and the author of *Diognetus*, testify that the Pauline discussion of justification involves more than a view of the law as "boundary markers." All three authors believe that justification by works refers to justification by good deeds, not identification as Jews through circumcision and food laws. They all place the discussion in soteriological categories. These three authors all confess that no one has obeyed the law perfectly. All have sinned, and this causes men to seek salvation in Christ. Justin explicitly states that the law requires perfect obedience, while the other two authors imply it. Once again, the NPP approach to this issue has no merit in the early fathers.

## FAITH AND WORKS

The NPP has called Luther's distinction between faith and works into question. If the Pauline polemic against the

---

13. Though, as noted above Justin does not postulate that Christ himself became a curse to do so as does Luther.

14. This point hasn't been specifically dealt with in detail throughout this study but it is highly significant that none of these figures, or in the vast reading I have done in the later patristic era, argue anything resembling this idea. Galatians 3:13 is never explicated as a description of Israel in exile.

15. There are of course several likely differences between Luther and the apostolic fathers. It is unclear whether these figures would agree with Luther that all of man's works are tainted by sin, and whether they would affirm Luther's approach to the radical depravity of mankind. However, the most prominent trajectories in Luther's theology of law are anticipated here.

Judaizers is about table fellowship rather than eternal salvation, then Paul did not argue against works righteousness as such. There is no strict faith/works dichotomy. This is also defended by several writers by arguing that πιστις Χριστου has been mistranslated as "faith in Christ," emphasizing the personal aspect of faith in Reformation theology; the correct translation, according to these writers, is "the faithfulness of Christ." Thus, the emphasis falls from individual salvation through justification apart from good deeds to a discussion of Christ and Torah in the covenant community.

It is in this context that a type of "covenantal nomism"[16] arises in Pauline interpretation. For Paul, salvation is a result of the grace of God initially. Entrance into the covenant is an act of God. However, good works are a necessary part of the covenant community. One must continue to be faithful to receive vindication at the resurrection. Works play a role in one's eschatological justification.[17] Thus any faith/works contrast in justification is manufactured.

Faith and works must always be kept separate in Luther's theology. They are both necessary aspects of the Christian life but play different roles. Faith alone justifies man before God. Works then serve as spontaneous acts of the Christian whose heart has been changed through the gospel. It was demonstrated that for Luther good works of the Christian are a result of alien righteousness, as is justification. Works are not the result of man's cooperation with God, or his own efforts. They flow from the indwelling presence of Christ in faith. Thus Christ is the true agent

---

16. Though Sanders admits both similarities and dissimilarities between Paul and covenantal nomism. For Sanders, Christ-mysticism differentiates the two theological systems; see his *Paul and Palestinian Judaism*, 511–14.

17. Whether Wright sees works as vindicating one on the last day, or showing the genuineness of faith and regeneration, is unclear.

*Conclusion*

of good works in the Christian. For Luther, covenantal nomism would be seen as a form of works righteousness. The Christian life is not only initiated through grace, but grace is effective through out.

Clement affirms Luther's faith/works distinction regarding justification.[18] Not only does Clement disassociate works from initial justification, but denies any justifying quality to works. This is why when he asks rhetorically, after explicating justification by faith alone, why one should do good works. Clement's answer demonstrates not that works serve to maintain one's covenant status or achieve eschatological vindication; rather he states, "For the Creator and Master of the universe himself rejoices in his works."[19] Clement upholds a faith/works distinction as would later become the central theme of Luther's theology.

Ignatius describes works in the Christian life in a manner synonymous with Luther. For Ignatius, works flow as a result of conversion and saving faith. He writes that "Faith cannot do the things of unfaithfulness, nor unfaithfulness the things of faith."[20] Like Luther, Ignatius emphasizes the analogy of a tree and its fruit. As a tree produces fruit, a Christian produces love and good works. It is the result of God's act of a changed nature that yields good works, not an attempt at maintaining one's covenant status, nor of achieving justification. Ignatius specifically speaks of eschatological vindication as being the result of the cross of Christ and faith, without mention of works. Ignatius is not a covenantal nomist.

There is not enough evidence in the *Epistle to Diognetus* to determine his precise view of good works and the law in the Christian life. However, what is clear is that there

18. *1 Clem.* 32:3–4.
19. *1 Clem.* 33:2.
20. Ignatius, *Eph.* 8:2.

is a distinction between faith and works. Good works in themselves are "unworthy" of bringing one into the kingdom of God. It is only through God's act of taking sin upon himself through Christ, and bringing Christ righteousness to sinners that men can be saved.

In Justin Martyr a soteriology appears that may bear some resemblance to covenantal nomism. While Justin certainly emphasizes grace and God's forgiveness, especially in the sacramental act of baptism, he does assign a meritorious place to works. As was shown above, he views one's own righteousness as necessary for eschatological vindication. For Justin, one is in the covenant by baptism through grace, and maintains this grace through obedience. The NPP proponents have an ally in Justin at this particular point.

## CONCLUSION

There are several significant agreements with Luther regarding Pauline interpretation in the first two centuries of the church. His doctrine of justification is supported by Clement, Ignatius, *Diognetus*, and somewhat in Justin. All of these figures place the Pauline polemic in the context of soteriology rather than ecclesiology. All of these figures are interested in personal salvation. Three of four writers describe the law as condemnatory. The law regards good works as such, not merely the Mosaic legislation given to Israel. None describe the law as Jewish "boundary markers." Justin Martyr explicitly states that the law requires perfect obedience, and that no one has rendered this obedience, leaving all of mankind under a curse. Three out of the four patristic theologians distinguish between faith and works in a Lutheran manner, and Ignatius and Clement describe works as the result of saving faith. Only in Justin is a NPP interpretation of works approached.

*Conclusion*

When historical theology is entered into the discussion, it becomes clear that Luther was not driven merely by medieval debates about righteousness and sin. In the first and second centuries, in a context far different from that of late medieval Europe, the most prominent themes in Luther's Pauline hermeneutic are already present. Perhaps rather than blaming the Lutheran tradition for misinterpreting Paul, New Testament scholars can begin to engage in exegesis that is historically informed, taking patristic thought and first- and second-century readings into account. When this is done with an eye to the Pauline text, Luther's reading may once again be vindicated.

# Bibliography

## PRIMARY SOURCES

*The Apostolic Fathers: Greek Texts and English Translations.* Edited and translated by Michael W. Holmes. Grand Rapids: Baker, 1992.

Holmes presents the best English translation of the apostolic fathers available. This is the translation I have used in my paper. Included is a critical Greek text along side of Holmes' English.

Justin, Martyr. *Dialogue avec Tryphon. Texte grec, traduction francaise, introduction, notes et index.* Edited by Georges Archambault. 2 vols. Textes et Documents 8, 11. Paris: Picard, 1909.

This is the critical edition of the Greek text of Justin's *Dialogue with Trypho*, which I have used. The introduction and notes are in French.

———. *S. Justini Apologiae duae.* Edited by Gerhard Rauschen. 2$^{nd}$ ed. FP 2. Bonn: Petri Hanstein, 1911.

Rauschen's is a twentieth-century critical edition of Justin's two apologetic treatises, which remains unsurpassed.

Justin, Martyr, et al. *The Apostolic Fathers, Justin Martyr, Irenaeus.* Ante-Nicene Fathers 1, 1st ser. Peabody, MA: Hendrickson, 1994.

The classic nineteenth-century Lightfoot translation of the apostolic fathers, Justin and Irenaeus, remains a valuable resource.

Luther, Martin. *Luther's Works*. Vol. 26, *Lectures on Galatians Chapters 1–4*, and vol. 27, *Lectures on Galatians Chapters 5–6*. Kindle ed. St. Louis: Concordia, 1962, 1964.

These volumes include both Luther's 1536 commentary on Galatians and his earlier lectures on Galatians. Reading the two in chronological order demonstrates the development of Luther's thought regarding justification.

## SECONDARY SOURCES

Bacon, Benjamin Wisner. "The Doctrine of Faith in Hebrews, James, and Clement of Rome." *Journal of Biblical Literature* 19/1 (1900) 12–21.

This article examines the discussions of faith in three early Christian epistles. He examines the use of Hebrews and James in Clement's writing. It is helpful in understanding how Clement utilized other canonical books in relation to his use of Paul.

Barnard, Leslie W. "The Background of St. Ignatius of Antioch." *Vigilae Christianae* 17 (1963) 193–206.

Barnard gives a helpful introduction to the figure of St. Ignatius, and gives the basics of the scholarly discussion around dating and authorship.

———. *Justin Martyr: His Life and Thought*. Cambridge: Cambridge University Press, 2008.

Any treatment of Justin's theology should take this book into account. Barnard has a very careful reading and explication of Justinian thought.

Barrett, C. K. "Jews and Judaizers in the Epistles of Ignatius." In *Jews, Greeks, and Christians*, edited by R. Hammerton Kelly and R. Scroggs, 220–44. Leiden: Brill, 1976.

Though not directly relating to the subject of justification, Barrett's article is a good resource for evaluating Ignatius' views on Judaism.

*Bibliography*

Barth, Karl. *The Epistle to the Romans*. Translated from the 6th ed. by Edwyn C. Hoskyns. Oxford: Oxford University Press, 1968.

Bornkamm, Gunther. *Paul*. Translated by D. M. G. Stalker. New York: Harper & Row, 1971.

Braaten, Carl E., and Robert W. Jenson, editors. *The Catholicity of the Reformation*. Grand Rapids: Eerdmans, 1996.

> The essays in this volume establish a connection between Luther and the previous medieval and patristic tradition. I follow the premise of the book that Luther's reformation is essentially continuous with previous church tradition.

———, editors. *Union with Christ: The New Finnish Interpretation of Luther*. Grand Rapids: Eerdmans, 1998.

> Unfortunately, most of the works in the Finnish school have not yet been translated in English. This volume addresses many of the issues that have not been dealt with in Mannermaa's two English volumes on Luther.

Buchanan, James. *The Doctrine of Justification: An Outline of Its History in the Church and of Its Exposition from Scripture*. Carlisle, PA: Banner of Truth, 1991.

> In this classic work on justification, James Buchanan briefly discusses patristic authors in connection with a Reformation understanding of justification.

Bultmann, Rudolph. *The Presence of Eternity: History and Eschatology*. New York: Harper, 1962.

———. *Theology of the New Testament*. Translated by Kendrick Grobel. 2nd ed. Waco, TX: Baylor University Press, 2007.

Carson, D. A., Peter T. O'Brien, and Mark A. Seifrid, editors. *Justification and Variegated Nomism*. 2 vols. WUNT 140, 181. Grand Rapids: Baker, 2001, 2004.

Chemnitz, Martin. *Examination of the Council of Trent*. Vol. 1. Translated by Fred Kramer. St. Louis: Concordia, 1971.

> This volume Martin Chemnitz's examination draws upon patristic sources extensively regarding the issue of justification. Several of his arguments, and quotes from which he draws, I find thoroughly convincing.

## Bibliography

Das, Andrew A. *Paul, the Law, and Covenant*. Peabody, MA: Hendrickson, 2001.

Davies, W. D. *Paul and Rabbinic Judaism: Some Rabbinic Elements in Pauline Theology*. 2nd ed. London: SPCK, 1958.

Dennison, William D. *The Young Bultmann: Context for His Understanding of God, 1884–1925*. American University Studies, ser. 7, Theology and Religion 241. New York: P. Lang, 2008.

Dunn, James D. G. *The New Perspective on Paul*. Grand Rapids: Eerdmans, 2007.

> This helpful volume gathers all of Dunn's articles relevant to the discussion of the New Perspective on Paul.

Faber, George Stanley. *The Primitive Doctrine of Justification Investigated: Relatively Related to the Several Definitions of the Church of Rome and the Church of England*. London: Seeley and Burnside, 1839.

> This nineteenth-century Anglican work is the most extensive attempt from a Protestant writer at showing the antiquity of the Protestant doctrine of justification. Though ultimately unconvincing, Faber gives a starting point for discussion of these issues.

Ferguson, Everett. *Baptism in the Early Church: History, Theology, and Liturgy in the First Five Centuries*. Grand Rapids: Eerdmans, 2009.

> The doctrine of baptism is essential for understanding both justification and grace in the early church, subsequent tradition in the middle ages, as well as Luther's appropriation of patristic thought. This is the best volume on the subject of baptism in the early church that I have come across.

Gaffin, Richard B., Jr. *Resurrection and Redemption: A Study in Paul's Soteriology*. 2nd ed. Phillipsburg, NJ: P & R 1987.

Gathercole, Simon J. *Where Is Boasting?: Early Jewish Soteriology and Paul's Response in Romans 1–5*. Grand Rapids: Eerdmans, 2002.

*Bibliography*

Hoenecke, Adolf. *Evangelical Lutheran Dogmatics.* Vol. 3. Milwaukee: Northwestern, 2003.

Jeffery, Steve, Michael Ovey, and Andrew Sach. *Pierced for Our Transgressions: Rediscovering the Glory of Penal Substitution.* London: Intervarsity, 2007.

Juntunen, Sammeli. "Luther and Metaphysics." In *Union with Christ,* edited by Carl E. Braaten and Robert W. Jenson, 129–56. Grand Rapids: Eerdmans, 1998.

Karkkainen, Veli-Matti. *One with God: Salvation as Deification and Justification.* Collegeville, MN: Liturgical, 2005.

> Though not primarily a work of historical theology, Karkkainen discusses the issue of deification with reference to the Finnish interpretation of Luther, giving practical implications of Luther's view.

Kelly, J. N. D. *Early Christian Doctrines.* Peabody, MA: Hendrickson, 2007.

> Kelly's work remains standard as a starting point for any patristic study. His comments on soteriology and law in the church fathers must be dealt with in this discussion.

King, David T., and William Webster. *Holy Scripture, the Ground and Pillar of Our Faith.* 3 vols. Battle Ground, WA: Christian Resources, 2001.

Lotz, David W. *Ritschl & Luther: A Fresh Perspective on Albrecht Rischl's Theology in Light of his Luther Study.* Nashville: Abingdon, 1974.

MacQuarrie, John. *An Existentialist Theology: A Comparison of Heidegger and Bultmann.* New York: Harper, 1955.

Mannermaa, Tuomo. *Christ Present in Faith: Luther's View of Justification.* Edited by Kirsi I. Stjerna. Minneapolis: Fortress, 2005.

> This is the main text supporting the Finnish interpretation of Luther. Mannermaa's work continues to be a great resource for reevaluating the doctrine of justification in Luther's thought.

———. "Justification and Theosis in Lutheran-Orthodox Perspective." In *Union with Christ: The New Finnish*

*Interpretation of Luther*, edited by Carl E. Braaten and Robert W. Jenson, 25–41. Grand Rapids: Eerdmans, 1998.

———. *Two Kinds of Love: Martin Luther's Religious World*. Translated by Kirsi I. Stjerna. Minneapolis: Fortress, 2010.

This second translated volume of Mannermaa's expands upon his previous thesis by expounding upon Luther's view of love in light of his proposed understanding of justification and *theosis*.

———. "Why Is Luther so Fascinating?: Modern Finnish Luther Research." In *Union with Christ: The New Finnish Interpretation of Luther*, edited by Carl E. Braaten and Robert W. Jenson, 1–20. Grand Rapids: Eerdmans, 1998.

Marquart, Kurt. "Luther and Theosis." *Concordia Theological Quarterly* 64/3 (2000) 182–205.

Mayer, Herbert T. "Clement of Rome and His Use of Scripture." *Concordia Theological Monthly* 42/9 (1971) 536–40.

Mayer examines the books of Scripture used by Clement, as well as his exegetical method of both Old and New Testament books.

McCain, Paul T., editor. *Concordia: The Lutheran Confessions*. St. Louis: Concordia, 2006.

McGrath, Alister E. "Forerunners of the Reformation?: A Critical Examination of the Evidence for Precursors of the Reformation Doctrines of Justification." *Harvard Theological Review* 75/2 (1982) 219–42.

McGrath analyses several pre-Reformation figures with the Protestant view of justification. He concludes that, while there are certain parallels, a "Lutheran" view of justification is new at the Reformation.

———. *Iustitia Dei: A History of the Christian Doctrine of Justification*. 3$^{rd}$ ed. Cambridge: Cambridge University Press, 2005.

This brilliant volume gives an in-depth overview of the doctrine of justification from Luther through the twentieth century. However, the first four centuries of the church remain virtually untouched.

———. "'The Righteousness of God' from Augustine to Luther." *Studia Theologica* 36 (1982) 63–78.

McGrath shows that while Luther was influenced by certain Augustinian ideas, the two figures differed on justification. For Augustine, it is a process dependent upon infused righteousness. The pre-Augustinian figures are not dealt with.

Molland, Einar. "The Heretics Combatted by Ignatius of Antioch." *Journal of Ecclesiastical History* 5 (1954) 1–6.

Molland studies early Christian heresies, and their interpretation and errors in the writings of Ignatius. This is helpful for any understanding of Ignatius' thought, as his letters are thoroughly polemical.

Muller, Richard A. *Post-Reformation Reformed Dogmatics: The Rise and Development of Reformed Orthodoxy, ca. 1520 to ca. 1725.* 4 vols. 2nd ed. Grand Rapids: Baker, 2003.

Needham, Nick. "Justification in the Early Church Fathers." In *Justification in Perspective: Historical Developments and Contemporary Challenges*, edited by Bruce L. McCormack et al., 25–53. Grand Rapids: Baker, 2006.

In this important article, Needham shows that many church fathers used the term "justification" in a legal sense. Though merit theology slowly developed in the West, Eastern figures were able to speak of the non-imputation of sin and imputation of righteousness in justification.

Nielson, Charles Merritt. "Clement of Rome and Moralism." *Church History* 31 (1962) 131–50.

Nielson discusses Clement of Rome's seeming adoption of *sola fide*, and his inescapable moralistic focus. He concludes that Clement's theology is inconsistent and contradictory.

## Bibliography

Nunn, H. P. V. "The Background of the Epistle of Clement of Rome." *Evangelical Quarterly* 18/1 (1946) 9–45.

> Nunn gives a helpful background to Clements epistle, his place in the church, and the situation of the Corinthians in the late first century.

Oberman, Heiko A. *The Dawn of the Reformation: Essays in Late Medieval and Early Reformation Thought*. Grand Rapids: Eerdmans, 1994.

Oden, Thomas C. *The Justification Reader*. Grand Rapids: Eerdmans, 2002.

> Oden proposes, in this volume, that there is a consensus among the fathers that salvation comes by grace through faith alone. He attempts to demonstrate this through several quotes from patristic sources and comparing them to Reformation confessions.

Parvis, Sarah, and Paul Foster, editors. *Justin Martyr and His Worlds*. Minneapolis: Fortress, 2007.

> This contains several essays on the background, history, and theology of Justin Martyr. It is an invaluable resource for any further study of Justin.

Pelikan, Jaroslav. *The Emergence of the Catholic Tradition*. Chicago: University of Chicago Press, 1971.

> Pelikan's classic series is valuable for the discussion of soteriology in the early church, as it is for studying virtually any patristic doctrine. Though soteriology is not the main thrust of his writing, what he does discuss on the topic is insightful.

Pieper, Franz. *Christian Dogmatics*. Vol. 2. St. Louis: Concordia, 1968.

Piper, John. *The Future of Justification: A Response to N. T. Wright*. Wheaton, IL: Crossway, 2007.

Quasten, Johannes. *Patrology*. 4 vols. Notre Dame: Christian Classics, 1986.

> Quasten's four-volume work details the life and work of every major Christian writer in the first five centuries, including giving the best critical texts of their works. This is the best available resource of its kind in English.

# Bibliography

Ridderbos, Herman N. *Paul: An Outline of His Theology*. Translated by John Richard de Witt. Grand Rapids: Eerdmans, 1997.

Robinson, John A. T. *Redating the New Testament*. Eugene, OR: Wipf and Stock, 2001.

Saarnivaara, Uuras. *Luther Discovers the Gospel: New Light upon Luther's Way from Medieval Catholicism to Evangelical Faith*. St. Louis: Concordia, 2005.

Sanders, E. P. *Paul and Palestinian Judaism: A Comparison of Patterns of Religion*. Philadelphia: Fortress, 1977.

Schoedel, W. R. "Are the Letters of Ignatius of Antioch Authentic?" *Religious Studies Review* 6 (1980) 196–201.

Schreiner, Thomas R. *The Law and Its Fulfillment: A Pauline Theology of Law*. Grand Rapids: Baker, 1998.

Seifrid, Mark A. *Christ Our Righteousness: Paul's Theology of Justification*. New Studies in Biblical Theology 9. Downers Grove, IL: InterVarsity, 2001.

———. "Righteousness Language in the Hebrew Scriptures and Early Judaism." In *Justification and Variegated Nomism*, edited by D. A. Carson, Peter T. O'Brien, and Mark A. Seifrid, 1:415–32. WUNT 140. Grand Rapids: Baker, 2001.

Skarsaune, Oskar. "Justin and His Bible." In *Justin Martyr and His Worlds*, edited by Sarah Parvis and Paul Foster. Minneapolis: Fortress, 2007.

Stendahl, Krister. *Paul Among Jews and Gentiles, and Other Essays*. Philadelphia: Fortress, 1976.

> This volume contains all of Stendahl's essays relating to Paulinism and Luther's supposed misreading of Paul through his introspective conscience. Any study of the NPP should start here.

Stylianopoulos, Theodore G. *Justin Martyr and the Mosaic Law*. SBLDS 20. Missoula, MT: Scholars, 1975.

Sungenis, Robert A. *Not by Scripture Alone: A Catholic Critique of the Protestant Doctrine of Sola Scriptura*. Santa Barbara, CA: Queenship, 1997.

Thielman, Frank. *From Plight to Solution: A Jewish Framework for Understanding Paul's View of the Law in Galatians and Romans*. Eugene, OR: Wipf and Stock, 2008.

———. *Paul & the Law: A Contextual Approach*. Downers Grove, IL: InterVarsity, 1995.

Torrance, Thomas F. *The Doctrine of Grace in the Apostolic Fathers*. Eugene, OR: Wipf and Stock, 1996.

> Torrance's study is a thorough and exegetical examination of the soteriology of the apostolic fathers. Though I remain unconvinced of many of his interpretations, no study on the issue can ignore this work.

Turner, H. E. W. *The Patristic Doctrine of Redemption: A Study of the Development of Doctrine During the First Five Centuries*. Eugene, OR: Wipf and Stock, 2004.

> With a lack of soteriological study in the pre-Augustinian church fathers, this work comes as a breath of fresh air. Turner discusses redemption from the first- to the fifth-century patristic sources.

VanHoozer, Kevin J. *Is There a Meaning in This Text?: The Bible, the Reader, and the Morality of Literary Knowledge*. Grand Rapids: Zondervan, 1998.

Vlachos, Chris A. *The Law and the Knowledge of Good & Evil: The Edenic Background of the Catalytic Operation of the Law in Paul*. Eugene, OR: Pickwick, 2009.

Westerholm, Stephen. *Perspectives Old and New on Paul: The "Lutheran" Paul and His Critics*. Grand Rapids: Eerdmans, 2004.

> This remains one of the best responses to the NPP from a broadly "Lutheran" perspective. His exegetical arguments are thoroughly convincing.

White, James R. *Scripture Alone: Exploring the Bible's Accuracy, Authority, and Authenticity*. Bloomington, MN: Bethany, 2004.

Williams, D. H. "Justification by Faith: A Patristic Doctrine." *Journal of Ecclesiastical History* 57/4 (2006) 649–67.

> Williams argues that, contrary to much scholarship, there is a ground for proposing that the early church taught *sola fide*. He argues that several Greek writers, especially Hilary, taught *sola fide* in some sense.

*Bibliography*

Wilson-Kastner, Patricia. "Andreas Osiander's Theology of Grace in the Perspective of the Influence of Augustine of Hippo." *Sixteenth Century Journal* 10/2 (1972) 72–91.

Wingren, Gustaf. *Man and the Incarnation: A Study in the Biblical Theology of Irenaeus*. Translated by Ross Mackenzie. Eugene, OR: Wipf and Stock, 2004.

Wolfson, Harry Austryn. *The Philosophy of the Church Fathers*. Vol. 1, *Faith, Trinity, Incarnation*. Cambridge, MA: Harvard University Press, 1956.

Wright, N. T. *The Climax of the Covenant: Christ and the Law in Pauline Theology*. Minneapolis: Fortress, 1993.

———. *Justification: God's Plan and Paul's Vision*. Downers Grove, IL: InterVarsity, 2009.

> In his most recent book on the subject, Wright challenges John Piper's book-length critique of his views. Wright defends his perspective both exegetically and theologically.

———. *The New Testament and the People of God*. Vol. 1 of *Christian Origins and the Question of God*. Minneapolis: Fortress, 1992.

———. *Paul: In Fresh Perspective*. Minneapolis: Fortress, 2005.

> This volume is comprised of a series of lectures delivered by Wright on the teaching of Paul. It expands upon his earlier work on the subject.

———. *What Saint Paul Really Said: Was Paul of Tarsus the Real Founder of Christianity?*. Grand Rapids: Eerdmans, 1997.

> This is Wright's first book on Paul. This is what brought the NPP discussion beyond the realm of the scholar into popular discussion.

Young, Norman J. *History and Existential Theology: The Role of History in the Thought of Rudolf Bultmann*. Philadelphia: Westminster, 1969.

www.ingramcontent.com/pod-product-compliance
Lightning Source LLC
Chambersburg PA
CBHW072144160426
43197CB00012B/2232